ANTI-CIVILIZATION

ANTI-CIVILIZATION

The Collapse of Society & the Case for the Common Good

ÉTIENNE-ALEXANDRE BEAUREGARD

SUTHERLAND HOUSE

TORONTO, 2026

Sutherland House
416 Moore Ave., Suite 304
Toronto, ON M4G 1C9

Copyright © 2026 Étienne-Alexandre Beauregard

All rights reserved, including the right to reproduce this book or portions thereof in any form whatsoever. For information on rights and permissions or to request a special discount for bulk purchases, please contact Sutherland House at sutherlandhousebooks@gmail.com

Sutherland House and logo are registered trademarks of The Sutherland House Inc.

First edition, August 2026

If you are interested in inviting one of our authors to a live event or media appearance, please contact sranasinghe@sutherlandhousebooks.com and visit our website at sutherlandhousebooks.com for more information.

We acknowledge the support of the Government of Canada.

Manufactured in Canada
Cover designed by Leah Ciani and Jordan Lunn
Book composed by Karl Hunt

Library and Archives Canada Cataloguing in Publication
Title: Anti-civilization : the collapse of society and the case for the common good / Étienne-Alexandre Beauregard.
Names: Beauregard, Étienne-Alexandre, editor.
Description: First edition. | Includes bibliographical references.
Identifiers: Canadiana (print) 20260172758 | Canadiana (ebook) 20260172790 | ISBN 9781997701668 (softcover) | ISBN 9781997701675 (EPUB) Subjects: LCSH: Common good. | LCSH: Civilization, Western. | LCSH: Generation Z.
Classification: LCC JC330.15 .B43 2026 |
DDC 320.01/1—dc23

ISBN 978-1-997701-66-8
eBook ISBN 978-1-997701-67-5

CONTENTS

Introduction

OVER THE PAST DECADE, the notion of decadence has resurfaced in the West. Although prophets of decline have long been ridiculed in some quarters, their diagnosis has been widely validated in intellectual circles and, above all, in the popular consciousness. On a civilizational scale, we are living through a "return of decadence" after an initial contemporary wave in the 1980s,[1] in the aftermath of the radical sixties. The sources of consternation remain the same. As early as 1983, the great French philosopher Raymond Aron wondered in his memoirs "whether the flourishing of freedoms, pluralism of beliefs, and individualistic hedonism are not jeopardizing the coherence of societies and their capacity for action," and how to "cement the unity of societies that are falling apart."[2] On the left of the political spectrum, intellectuals such as Jacques Julliard made the same diagnosis with respect to France's decline: "the result of rampant individualism and the failure of the elites, calls into question the social contract itself."[3] Crisis of unity, crisis of norms, crisis of values—all these terms describe the collapse of our collective ideals, including democracy, which seems more fragile than ever as political elites now look at ordinary people with suspicion.

This dynamic came into play at the end of the postwar economic boom, in the tumultuous years that saw the birth of the radical sixties, the May '68 movement, and many other protests that called for the replacement of an "old order" deemed oppressive and conformist, by an alleged reign of freedom. In hindsight, the upheavals that swept the West in these years resemble a transition from one way of life to another. The society that the protesters wanted to leave behind was a thriving social democracy, made possible by a certain unity, cemented by low immigration and vigorous assimilation, and more generally by strong social norms aligned with a conformist majority.[4] American sociologist Robert Putnam refers to this unity as a "great convergence."[5] French pollster Jérôme Fourquet describes a "homogenization of French society through standardized lifestyles and consumption."[6] The rise of a consumer society brought the West closer to the democratic, unitary, and republican ideal of a nation with common references and a widely shared lifestyle, where the middle class had become the cultural benchmark. In many ways, this model represents the peaceful fulfillment of the democratic ideal of the Atlantic Revolutions of the eighteenth century, which was built on praise for the majority and the desire for the people to govern themselves. The silent generation, which preceded the baby boomers, embodied this culture of normality: more conservative and conformist than previous and subsequent generations, they married younger and had more children, had a low suicide rate, and reported high levels of happiness.[7] In the United States, this era was defined by the figure of the "common man," admired as the symbol of an optimistic society, notably by Franklin Roosevelt's vice president, Henry Wallace, who in 1942 prophesied the "century of the common man."[8] However, this heyday of Western civilization ultimately lasted only about thirty years before turning against itself and beginning its own deconstruction.

The history of our time is one of accelerating social change, which threatens the transmission of values within Western nations and fosters understandable alienation among the majority of citizens.[9]

There is a real sense of mourning among older people, who see the lack of intergenerational continuity and feel that they are living in a world different from that of their children or grandchildren. Among younger generations, the situation is hardly more encouraging. More and more "suffer from existential emptiness, feel that they were born in the midst of a disordered era, in a world without roots, a civilization in ruins," prey to "the same thirst for ideals, the same desire for a conversion with no turning back to a belief that would give meaning to their existence, that would allow them to rebuild themselves, to overcome the abyss of nihilism."[10] Behind the growing polarization and rise of extremism that particularly afflicts young people, there is a desire for roots, "the most important and least recognized need of the human soul."[11] This need is cruelly undermined in a civilization that increasingly compromises its unity and cohesion in the name of individuality and authenticity.

What Is Civilization?

According to sociologist Norbert Elias, civilization is first and foremost a process of pacifying customs and relationships between individuals.[12] It brings order out of chaos by ending the unrestrained, violent, and precarious state of nature in which man obeys no law higher than himself. Thanks to the growing interdependence of human beings and their increasing self-control, it leads to the management of impulses that are harmful to social peace. The modern state, with its monopoly on legitimate violence, is the centerpiece of this process, the Leviathan imagined by Hobbes, which has the necessary force to compel everyone to restrain their bad instincts under penalty of punishment. It formally enshrines in institutions of state an organic process that was already taking place on a smaller scale in families, villages, and communities. However, Elias tells us that as civilization progresses, it is no longer fear of coercion that motivates everyone to respect the common law, but self-control. It is Kant's autonomy of the will or Freud's superego, through which the individual identifies with the law and makes it his own. In other words, the process of civilization is one through which human beings realize that they have an objective advantage in subordinating their interests to those of the community, because this surrender brings them peace, security, and fulfillment. This fundamental observation is also shared by the great social contract theorists who inspired the modern revolutions, namely Locke, Hobbes, and Rousseau. Civilization is therefore only possible thanks to what Robert Putnam calls social capital, or "social networks and the associated norms of reciprocity and trustworthiness."[13] Even for those who do not participate directly, there are substantial advantages to living in a society where there is a high degree of cohesion among members, as this guarantees security and solidarity. Informal rules such as social norms, as well as coercive laws, are essential to the building of social capital, and they can only be deconstructed at the expense of the public good.

Since the end of the postwar economic boom, the process of civilization stimulated by the "great convergence" earlier in the twentieth century seems to have stalled, or even regressed. Could this decline be the perverse consequence of Western nations' success in integrating the vast majority of citizens economically and culturally through social democratic compromise, which distributed prosperity as never before? *The New York Times* columnist Ross Douthat suggests this theory in *The Decadent Society*, describing decadence as the coexistence of high material prosperity with moral and cultural stagnation.[14] At the turn of the 1970s, American political scientist Ronald Inglehart described a shift from materialistic values, such as personal and financial security, societal stability, and respect for the law, to post-materialistic values, such as personal emancipation, creativity, and environmental protection.[15] Following the logic of

Maslow's pyramid, the West turned to post-materialism once the material needs of the majority of citizens had been met. Nevertheless, current political upheavals force us to realize that there is an irreconcilable tension between these two processes and that a civilization committed to post-materialism unwittingly deconstructs the social capital essential to its survival, reproducing the opposite of the process of civilization described by Elias, namely the liberation of impulses and the breakdown of interdependence between citizens. This process of *anti-civilization* is the topic of this book.

A Seismic Shift in Modernity

We are currently facing a major change of course in modernity, illustrated by its relationship with the figure of the people and its corollaries, the majority and the common man. Once integral to the French and American revolutions, these concepts at the heart of the democratic ideal have fallen from their pedestal, discredited by totalitarian regimes that have carried out their dictatorial and murderous designs in the name of the people, but also against them. Contemporary democracy therefore experiences a persistent unease with the law of the majority, now wrongly associated with the "darkest hours" of our recent history. Chapter 1 will thus show how mistrust of ordinary people has taken center stage in our democracies, opening the door to an individualistic drift cloaked in false anti-fascism.

In response to the totalitarian nightmare, the second half of the twentieth century saw the rise of a "negative" conception of freedom, theorized notably by Isaiah Berlin, which pits freedom of the individual against the society and nation that surround him, shaping an ideal of autonomy that eventually leads to an exit from the social contract. This singular way of thinking about freedom, the subject of Chapter 2, leaves room for antisocial impulses in areas such as drug use, crime, and sexuality, and has damaging consequences for the most vulnerable as it protects the misbehavior of the powerful. Another contemporary perversion of liberalism, the ethic of authenticity, as defined by thinkers such as Charles Taylor, exalts individual differences as the foundation of personal identity, explicitly breaking with the national identity and the characteristics shared by the majority. It now tends toward a new conformism of difference, described in Chapter 3, which undermines social cohesion by deconstructing the duty of integration into the nation that is necessary in a peaceful democracy.

The post-materialist shift and the end of the class struggle between the bourgeoisie and the proletariat at the turn of the 1960s and 1970s also had major consequences for the political left, as described in Chapter 4. Herbert Marcuse's thinking, seeking to save critical theory from its predicted demise, initiated a redeployment of the Marxist matrix around so-called marginalized identity groups in order to deconstruct the common norms of the polity. Rather than saving the left, this doctrinal renewal paradoxically accelerated its decline, pushing more and more groups to the right as they became integrated into the core of society and excluded from the "margins," repelled by increasing radicalism. Populism, now ubiquitous in our political life, must be understood as a reaction to a "revolt of the elites"[16] on the left, whose political base is now the "enlightened" fraction of the population that holds a university degree. Chapter 5 will describe this major sociological shift among Western elites, as well as how it corrodes the foundations of representative democracy. As their values are marginalized in elite circles, the middle classes are turning to a populist right, which has begun a necessary ideological shift in a context that no longer has anything to do with the Cold War and the fight against communism.

While populism has the great virtue of reintroducing the figure of the majority and the more conservative values of the middle classes into the public sphere, it is not immune to excesses that can prove as harmful to civilization as the progressivism it opposes; these excesses will be described in Chapter 6. Chapter 7 will then propose a conservatism focused on the common good and the reconstruction of a coherent society around the figure of the nation. The task facing conservatives today is to turn the page on critical theories of the social order in order to return to a healthy culture of normality. It is no longer a question of pushing freedom ever further against communist tyranny, but rather of renewing the civilizing conditions that allowed freedom to blossom and be maintained during the era of democratic revolutions, now weakened by a spirit of negation that has perverted the noble ideal of freedom and, with it, Western consciousness. To achieve this, it is imperative to place our trust once again in the nation and the majority, and through them in the common good.

CHAPTER 1

The Fall of the Common Man

BEFORE THE WEST'S SHIFT toward anti-civilization, liberal democracy was framed by what could be called a "culture of normality," stemming from the democratic revolutions of the eighteenth century. Absolutism gave way to democracy primarily because people believed in the wisdom of the common man and his ability to govern himself through majority rule. However, the experience of totalitarianism, and in particular a certain interpretation of the Holocaust, called into question the foundations of Western democratic thinking by raising the question of the banality of evil. What if radical evil were the work of the common man? What if the people were dangerous? It is through this misconception that Western values have turned against themselves.

Democratic Revolutions and the Culture of Normality

To legitimize the transfer of power from a monarch to the majority, it was necessary to praise the virtues of the humble and the wisdom of the masses. Jean-Jacques Rousseau, the French revolutionaries' favorite philosopher, became an apologist for the people in his *Social Contract*, mainly through his conception of the general will: "the general will is always right and always tends to the public good," which "alone can direct the forces of the State according to the object of its founding, which is the common good." In his view, the people are never wrong, and when they appear to be mistaken, it is because they have been deceived, not because they are corrupt.[1] Emmanuel-Joseph Sieyès, in his eulogy to the Third Estate (the social class comprising everyone who was neither clergy nor nobility), defends this people who are "everything," "a strong, robust man with one arm in chains," while "the privileged, far from being useful to the Nation, can only weaken and harm it."[2] The claims of the Third Estate are based precisely on its normality and its majority status, for this class is "the totality of citizens belonging to the common order"[3] and who support the nation through their labor. It is because it is a net contributor to the well-being of the whole and because it submits to the same rules as everyone else that the Third Estate earns its dignity and deserves to govern itself. This blind faith in the general will, and in those who speak in its name, came with its own perils as it paved the way for Robespierre, architect of the Reign of Terror, but it nonetheless illustrates the spirit on which modern democracies were built: government by the majority rather than by an aristocratic elite.

In a more moderate form, this majority sensibility was also present in John Locke, the father of British liberalism, for whom supreme power ultimately belongs to the majority: "And thus every man, by consenting with others to make one body politic under one government, puts himself under an obligation to every one of that society to submit to the determination of the majority, and to be concluded by it; or else this original compact, whereby he with others incorporates into one society, would signify nothing."[4] Although he is known as the thinker of natural freedoms, Locke is nonetheless imbued with democratic imagination and the culture of normality; according to his political philosophy, the people remain the only ones empowered to draw the limits of individual rights and remain at all times the depositaries of sovereignty, which is why they hold the right to revolt against bad government.[5] His conception of tolerance is also marked by the majority principle, which gives priority to the maintenance of a certain social order over the expression of individuality.[6] For Locke, as for the founding fathers of the United States, freedom is not license, and the devolution of power to the people depends on the virtue of the latter. James Madison, author of the American Bill of Rights, argued that "to suppose that any form of government will secure liberty or happiness without any virtue in the people, is a chimerical idea."[7] This doctrine, which sees no public virtue without private virtue, is diametrically opposed to the liberal orthodoxy of the late twentieth century, which argues, on the contrary, that the common good is never approached as closely as when citizens believe they are pursuing their individual interests without particular concern for the good.

Democracy thus emerged through a conception of freedom based on self-control, derived from Christianity and secularized by Immanuel Kant. This freedom values "the universal imperative of duty"[8] over one's own individual inclinations. Since the will is not always subject to the laws of reason, man must force himself to make his individual will compatible with objective laws: he must embrace the common good and apply it to himself. Sigmund Freud, in *Civilization and Its Discontents*, formulates the same dualism in another way: "in consequence of this primary mutual hostility of human beings, civilized society is perpetually threatened with disintegration," so "human life in common is only made possible when a majority comes together which is stronger than any separate individual and which remains united against all separate individuals."[9]

Social norms, the superego of society, must impose on the individual "strict ideal demands, disobedience to which is visited with 'fear of conscience,'"[10] in order to preserve an orderly polity. For Norbert Elias, this is the very foundation of the principle of civilization: to live in peace, individuals must develop a sense of self-restraint, integrating into their own conscience the renunciation of brutality and force expressed by the state's monopoly on legitimate violence.[11] We can therefore see that before the 1960s and 1970s, democracy coexisted harmoniously with what Gilles Lipovetsky calls a "secular religion of duty." Democratic revolutions broke with absolutism, but not with "the moral tradition of self-renunciation," which instead transformed into "unconditional duties towards oneself, towards others, and towards the community."[12] The founding democratic ideal of modernity is thus closer to a balance between two competing principles than to the outright triumph of freedom over authority, an overly Manichean view that omits that these two principles have coexisted for a long time.[13]

According to Robert Putnam, this culture of normality was particularly dominant in the first half of the twentieth century, with the idealization of the figure of the "common man," a powerful cultural symbol of national solidarity and social equality.[14] During the postwar economic boom, widespread enrichment in Western countries led to the emergence of a strong middle class, which became the cultural reference point in most nations. Like Sieyès' Third Estate, the middle class is "everything"; it "embodies the values of society as a whole" and is at the center of the collective consciousness, both for the ruling classes, who must take its preferences into account, and for immigrants, who dream of assimilating into it.[15] Before the imperative of differentiation took over, it was not uncommon for newcomers to adapt their names to better integrate into the community: Dino Crocetti became Dean Martin in America; Shahnourh Aznavourian became Charles Aznavour in

France.[16] Such a requirement would seem brutal today, to be sure. Nevertheless, as recently as the last century, it was commonplace because the idealized status of the common man made people want to assimilate in this way, without resort to coercion.

While norms are changing and occasionally contested, the principle of normativity is not, and "its most important function is to maintain and reproduce a system of generalized trust."[17] This concept has two fundamental meanings. First, the norm as normativity refers to a perfectionist ideal and therefore consists of a judgment of how things should be: for example, health conceived as the total absence of disease represents a model that is rarely achieved in reality.[18] These unwritten rules, which vary from one society to another, are a kind of "soft law," which is not imposed by the state, but rather by the gaze of everyone and by the prevailing view of what is good in a given society. Furthermore, the norm as an ideal coexists with a second meaning, the norm as normality, or what is perceived as common or ordinary. This polysemy reinforces the culture of normality, where the perfectionist ideal that is never achieved merges with the ideal of normality within the group. The ordinary man and the middle class are therefore both determinants of normality and normativity: what is widespread is what we want to become. Although they no longer have a good reputation, norms were once the spearhead of integration, both social and cultural, into a shared ideal seen as essential to the preservation of democracy.

The Banality of Evil and the Disgrace of the Common Man

How did the common man, an emblematic figure of democracy for two centuries, fall from his pedestal? He was undermined alongside the democratic idea of the people by the totalitarian experience, and the unspeakable crimes committed in their name by tyrants: "Totalitarian regimes claim to represent them . . . and fight in their name, but by giving them this primary role, they burden them forever with all the evils of which they are guilty. Until now, the people were a promise; with totalitarianism, they become a mortal danger to societies and individuals."[19] The great trauma of the twentieth century, the tragic memory of the Holocaust, taints it more than any other excess, although unfairly. Let us not forget that Nazi Germany was a one-party dictatorship, and that the Germans never voted for Auschwitz. It was not immediately obvious that the average citizen was to blame for the Jewish genocide and the crimes of a murderous totalitarianism, yet this interpretation eventually prevailed in popular consciousness. Hannah Arendt's controversial 1963 book, *Eichmann in Jerusalem: A Report on the Banality of Evil*, can be seen to summarize this thesis of the Holocaust as a pathology of the common man.

A German Jewish philosopher who fled Nazism to take refuge in the United States, Arendt attended the 1961 trial in Jerusalem of Adolf Eichmann, a Nazi official considered to be the main architect of the Final Solution. At his trial, people expected to see a hardened criminal, a bloodthirsty butcher, but instead, a neat little official appeared before the jury, and his entire defense was based on the idea that he was just a cog in the machine, obeying orders without questioning them. Eichmann described himself as a law-abiding citizen who had "lived his whole life according to Kant's moral precepts, and especially according to a Kantian definition of duty,"[20] and his sole motivation was to obey orders, whatever they might be: "he would have had a bad conscience only if he had not done what he had been ordered to do—to ship millions of men, women, and children to their death with great zeal and the most meticulous care."[21] According to his defense, his actions were not anti-Semitic, as he had no personal opinions about the Final Solution. On the contrary, he stated that "he would have killed his own father if he had received an order to that effect,"[22] in order to absolve himself of any personal blame and attribute sole responsibility to the society that had made him.

The jury was not fooled, and Eichmann was sentenced to death. It must be said that during his exile in Argentina, Eichmann had given an interview about his role in the Final Solution, in which he declared himself to be "a conscientious bureaucrat, certainly . . . But this conscientious bureaucrat was inseparable from a fanatical fighter for the freedom of my blood and my race."[23] Far from being repentant and ignorant of his crimes, he boasted about them: "I will die happily, taking with me five million enemies of the Reich."[24] His defense before the court was therefore nothing more than a role he had written for himself, using the dominant ethics of the time to portray himself as a common man. However, Arendt buys into this defense, or at least uses it to guide humanity, which, in her view, no longer thinks to ask itself what makes normal, ordinary men into mass murderers.[25] From a philosophical standpoint, the question certainly is fascinating. However, extrapolating Eichmann's case to humanity as a whole is far from self-evident.

Describing the architect of the Holocaust as a simple-minded man who "never made a decision on his own, who was extremely careful always to be covered by orders, who . . . did not even like to volunteer suggestions and always required directives,"[26] she attributes the Jewish genocide to "sheer thoughtlessness"[27] and to men driven by a Kantian ethic of duty, who massacred 6 million of their fellow human beings without thinking about what they were doing. She paints a picture of a culture of normality gone mad, "the moral collapse . . . in respectable European society,"[28] which was led by a blind vision of duty to commit radical evil, incapable of questioning what it was doing. Through the banality of evil, Arendt makes the appalling diagnosis that questions the very legitimacy of norms:

> Evil in the Third Reich had lost the quality by which most people recognize it—the quality of temptation. Many Germans and many Nazis, probably an overwhelming majority of them, must have been tempted not to murder, not to rob, not to let their neighbors go off to their doom . . ., and not to become accomplices in all these crimes by benefiting from them. But, God knows, they had learned how to resist temptation.[29]

If it had happened to Eichmann, then it could have happened to anyone, and the problem of Nazism became, at the same time, that of the entire Western world. It mattered little that it was also the West that defeated Nazism and stopped the Holocaust. Indirectly, Arendt's thesis reinforced that of Theodor W. Adorno, who argued in *The Authoritarian Personality*[30] that the main culprit behind Nazism was ultimately the average man who was conservative, raised in a normal family and guided by an ethic of duty and respect for authority. This thesis had been developed as early as 1933 by Wilhelm Reich in his book *The Mass Psychology of Fascism*. Under the pretext of discovering the material conditions that gave rise to National Socialism, the Austrian psychiatrist blamed the traditional family, describing it as "the factory of [the] structure and ideology" of the authoritarian state.[31] The main culprit, he argued, was the father, who embodied authority and thus became "the state's most valuable tool.[32] He would instill in his children a respect for rules and teach his sons how to reproduce this dynamic of domination within their own families. At the heart of patriarchal oppression, Reich sees "mortal terror of natural sexuality," which reveals "one of the cornerstones of National Socialist ideology."[33] This imposed repression of sexual desire is at the heart of the alienation of workers and curbs their aspiration for freedom from early childhood: "Every child and adolescent goes through the struggle against the temptation to masturbate. In this struggle, all elements of the reactionary human structure develop."[34]

Economic liberation would therefore first require sexual liberation and, more broadly, the breakdown of old customs embodied in the family. Weakening the family would mean weakening the "central reactionary germ cell, the most important place of reproduction of the reactionary and conservative individual."[35] This doctrine is still present on the left, notably among sociologists such as Geoffroy de Lagasnerie, who denounces "the family [as] the main incubator of the ideological atmosphere of conservatism," which must be overcome in order to achieve civilization of liberty.[36] Mona Chollet also criticizes the "authoritarian" education of children as a way of "endorsing the dominant world order" and dismissing the idea that "social rules can be questioned and discussed."[37] The family system would therefore be an implicit pact between generations to perpetuate the repression of each individual's deepest desires:

> The implicit promise that society makes to you is that if you accept the abuse of power by your educators, you will be rewarded with the power you will one day have over your own children. After seeing your desires repressed, you will have the right to repress someone else's.[38]

The idea that the family and the ordinary man form a reactionary matrix that must be deconstructed is, in a way, the double negative of the conservative vision, which, on the contrary, sees the foundation of civilization in those *little platoons* dear to Edmund Burke:

> It is in the family, in local clubs and societies, in school, church, team, regiment and university that people learn to interact as free beings, each taking responsibility for his actions and accounting to his neighbour. When society is organised from above, either by the top-down government of a revolutionary dictatorship, or by the impersonal edicts of an inscrutable

> bureaucracy, then accountability rapidly disappears from the political order, and from society too.[39]

Conversely, the father plays a fundamental role in exposing the child to the norms of society that exist outside the family and preparing him to integrate the group when he is older, thus avoiding the misfortune of exclusion.[40] A sizeable amount of research also shows that the absence of a father is one of the most important predictors of poverty and crime. Thus, the family is not the incubator of fascism, but rather that of citizens who respect laws and norms, particularly impervious to the revolution desired by Marxist thinkers such as Adorno and Reich. Nevertheless, the rise of anti-family rhetoric foreshadowed the decline of the culture of normality, now equated with tyranny.

A New Vision of Tyranny

As the people were declared illegitimate in the name of the fight against totalitarianism, democratic theory began a paradigm shift and redefined the "enemy" against which it stood. Since the American and French revolutions were uprisings against absolute monarchies, the democratic theory that supported them was particularly wary of the misdeeds of rulers, and even more so of tyrants who concentrated all political power in their own hands. For Jean-Jacques Rousseau, the fact that a single individual was invested with supreme power inevitably led to corruption, because "the best kings wish to have the power to be wicked if they please, without ceasing to be masters," and "their personal interest is, in the first place, that the people should be weak and miserable, and should never be able to resist them."[41] Although John Locke was less categorical, he nevertheless considered that the legitimacy of the monarch depended on the fact that he considered "the good of the public the end of his government."

Conversely, when a king "makes all give way to his own will and appetite," the people are "absolved from any farther obedience"[42] to his rule. They therefore have the legitimacy to overthrow him and establish a new power in accordance with the common good. For both Rousseau and Locke, tyranny therefore refers to a regime that disregards the general will and exercises its power against it, in the interests of those who govern.

The totalitarian trauma and its false interpretation as a pathology of the common man have thus overturned democratic theory. From now on, the general will or the law of the majority can no longer be trusted, because they are held responsible for the worst crimes against humanity. Another strand of liberal theory, almost inaudible during the "century of the common man," replaced it: the "tyranny of the majority" became the main threat to democracy. John Stuart Mill is one of its most eloquent representatives. A defender of utopian and perfectionist liberalism, whose goal was the moral progress of humanity,[43] Mill was fundamentally distrustful of the people, whom he saw as embodying "collective mediocrity."[44] In *On Liberty*, he announced the changing face of tyranny, which was shifting from the sovereign to the people themselves:

> In time, however, a democratic republic came to occupy a large portion of the earth's surface, and made itself felt as one of the most powerful members of the community of nations; and elective and responsible government became subject to the observations and criticisms which wait upon a great existing fact. It was now perceived that such phrases as "self-government," and "the power of the people over themselves," do not express the true state of the case. The "people" who exercise the power are not always the same people with those over whom it is exercised; and the "self-government" spoken of is not the government of each by himself, but of each by all the rest. The will of the people,

> moreover, practically means the will of the most numerous or the most active part of the people; the majority, or those who succeed in making themselves accepted as the majority; the people, consequently may desire to oppress a part of their number; and precautions are as much needed against this as against any other abuse of power . . . in political speculations "the tyranny of the majority" is now generally included among the evils against which society requires to be on its guard.[45]

Ordinary people and the middle classes thus become objects of mistrust, because of bad instincts that they would never be able to completely suppress: "where there is the strong permanent leaven of intolerance in the feelings of a people, which at all times abides in the middle classes of this country, it needs but little to provoke them into actively persecuting those whom they have never ceased to think proper objects of persecution."[46] In the same way, traditions, even if they are useful for social cohesion, would be harmful to man because they do "not educate or develop in him any of the qualities which are the distinctive endowment of a human being," so that those who follow them "[have] no character, no more than a steam-engine has a character."[47] In Mill's writing, tradition and the presence of widely shared customs among a people become a "despotism of custom,"[48] an adversary of the human progress he desires. Against the sovereignty of the people in the political sphere, or of their customs in everyday life, Mill defends a maximalist individual sovereignty, according to which "the only purpose for which power can be rightfully exercised over any member of a civilised community, against his will, is to prevent harm to others."[49] He thus breaks with classical democratic theory focused on the common good, but also with one of the fundamental intuitions of conservatism, according to which customs and traditions represent a form of collective wisdom, an accumulation of knowledge transcending generations, far greater than what a single individual could discover on their own.[50]

This movement, which sees the majority and its traditions as the main face of tyranny, made a strong comeback in Western consciousness after World War II, notably with *The Open Society and Its Enemies* by Austrian philosopher Karl Popper. This work had a major impact, along with the idea of an "open society" whose primary objective eschews the common good or any form of general interest in favor of devoting itself entirely to "the right [of every man] to model his life himself, as far as this does not interfere too much with others,"[51] a reformulation of Mill's "harm principle." Through this individualistic prism, a democracy concerned with the common good and preserving the way of life of ordinary people is equated with the "tribalism" of closed societies, defined by "their magical or irrational attitude towards the customs of social life, and the corresponding rigidity of these customs."[52] The idea that the community is more than the sum of its parts and that social or cultural norms can take precedence over certain individual desires appears to Popper as "veiled forms of propaganda for a return to tribalism."[53] Starting from the prejudice that "all intolerance [arises] from dependence on an ideal,"[54] contemporary defenders of so-called tolerance conclude that the best way to live in a pluralistic society would be to deconstruct the ideals and norms that govern public life.

The "open society," based on the primacy of the individual over the people, leads to a substantial upheaval in democratic theory. In Popper's view, democracy as "government by the people" is an outdated concept, and a new democratic theory should not be based on the idea that majority rule is intrinsically good or just, but on the idea that tyranny is bad.[55] A democratic government is therefore one that is not authoritarian, that preserves civil liberties, and that can be peacefully dismissed. On the other hand, "the adoption of the democratic principle, thus defined, does not necessarily consider the decisions of the majority to be good. The majority is thus excluded from democratic theory, which is reoriented toward the promotion of an "open society" that challenges the culture of normality and the Kantian duty that had been widely accepted until then. There is therefore a paradox at the very heart of this theory, namely that the open society as imagined by Popper or Mill does not exist anywhere on Earth. No nation-state is a creation *ex nihilo* of abstract and autonomous individuals; rather, they are the political and institutional emanation of centuries-old cultural entities, even millennia-old in the case of the oldest peoples of Europe. While classical democratic theory respected this fundamental fact, hoping that the people could govern themselves without passing judgment on how they should do so, the open society is not an existing state of affairs to be defended against the onslaught of totalitarianism. Rather, it is a project to be built, which necessarily involves overcoming established customs and norms, now decried as tribalism and totalitarianism. In other words, the construction of Karl Popper's "open society" entails the deconstruction of Norbert Elias's "civilizing process."

The Ever-Shifting Definition of the "Far Right"

If the painful memory of totalitarianism has been hijacked to invalidate the classical theory of democracy, the same is true of the reference to the "far right" or fascism, which has long been misused. As a new beginning for European identity, 1945 left us with a guilty conscience and Nazism as the figure of radical evil in politics.[56] With totalitarian dictatorships fortunately gone in the Western world, our societies are no longer really fighting against the fall of democracy. As French socialist leader Lionel Jospin once said, they are instead engaged in an "anti-fascist theater," whose antagonists are tradition, the nation, or any principle that would restrict individual will. Popper calls these antagonists the "enemies" of open society. As Québec sociologist Mathieu Bock-Côté rightly points out, we are faced with an "elusive far right,"[57] a shifting fascism whose definition is periodically redefined. Fascism has fallen prey to "concept creep," and the indiscriminate use of a label so heavily loaded makes it lose its true meaning. Some, like Judith Butler, embrace this vagueness and claim the legitimacy to use it as they see fit, without any objective definition: "We would be wrong to think that all its possible forms have already existed and that we can call something 'fascist' only if it conforms to established models."[58]

Yale University philosopher Jason Stanley published *How Fascism Works* in 2018, sounding the alarm and echoing the clichés of the moment about the return of radical evil in politics. Its distinctive feature is said to be attachment to the figure of the nation, "a sense of group identity that is by its nature opposed to the cosmopolitan ethos and individualism of liberal democracy."[59] Consequently, the fear of becoming a cultural minority in one's own country or even the teaching of great works in schools would be signs of fascism, since they reinforce a majority national narrative that leaves insufficient room for minorities.[60] Beyond the question of identity, political discourse focused on "law and order" or the defense of the value of work would also be fascist, as would the denunciation of "the wrongs a globalized economy does to rural areas, adding to it a focus on traditional rural values of self-sufficiency supposedly put at risk by the success of liberal cities culturally and economically."[61] Among contemporary "anti-fascists," it is no longer the historical figure of Hitlerian or Mussolinian totalitarianism that is being fought, but rather critics of fashionable progressivism, particularly those who remain attached to national roots and reject the shift toward the "open society" in the making since the end of the twentieth century.

This concept creep explains why those who bear the infamous stigma often have no connection with the historical far right, the heir to actual fascism. Even representatives of the institutional right who are perceived as too conservative, such as Stephen Harper in Canada or Boris Johnson in the United Kingdom, have tasted this ostracism at one time or another. They have in common the "sin" of having addressed cultural and security issues rather than confining themselves solely to economic management. The demonization of national conservatism thus serves as a warning to all players in the political game: if they speak out on identity issues, they will be punished in turn. In France, the patriotic and republican left is also attacked when it dares to talk about the people and the nation. Citing Jean-Pierre Chevènement, Régis Debray, Manuel Valls, and even Jean-Luc Mélenchon's 2017 campaign, political scientist Philippe Marlière argues that France is witnessing a "refocusing of the critical left towards a form of cultural nationalism usually claimed by reactionary right-wing movements."[62] He criticizes them for adhering to a "communitarian" vision of the nation, in that it "expects citizens to adhere to a national narrative, norms, and values specific to this community."[63] Behind this accusation lies a condemnation of French republicanism, a modern doctrine if ever there was one, but one that still gives an important role to the nation. To be a legitimate and anti-fascist interlocutor, it is essential to avoid "issues so deeply contaminated by the far right"[64] such as security, immigration, secularism, and the nation. This speaks volumes about the perception of the patriotic left among progressives, who believe it to be consciously preparing the return of the "far right." Actually, this ideological intolerance reveals what they are really fighting against: mostly the nation-state.

American academic Paul Gottfried points out that framing fascism as a "radicalized right" and, consequently, antifascism as a left-wing project, was not always self-evident.[65] The right also has its history of fighting fascism, with Winston Churchill and Charles de Gaulle being the most admirable examples. Nevertheless, Stalin's USSR and communist intellectuals appropriated anti-fascism and turned it into an object of propaganda, which has rarely been challenged since. It should be remembered that the Berlin Wall was officially called the "Anti-Fascist Protection Rampart" by the Soviet regime, even though everyone knew that it served to prevent East Germans from fleeing to the free world. Against this misleading narrative, a genuine critique of fascism, based on historical reality rather than ideological fabrication, must necessarily recognize the revolutionary nature of fascism. As historian Johann Chapoutot explains, the Third Reich was both revolutionary and reactionary, insofar as it assumed that "the Germanic race has, since its origins, been alienated and denatured by cultural and biological influences from elsewhere, which are slowly destroying it and will soon cause it to disappear."[66] Christian humanism was the first among these alienating influences, as it recognized the dignity of the weak and was viscerally opposed to eugenics. To make the Nazi program acceptable to the Germans, the regime embarked on an "archaeological operation" aimed at substituting one normative system for another, a racial "refoundation" that sought to "return to the instinct of the race, which, simply following its natural intuition, acted in accordance with nature," before it was altered by Christian morality.[67]

Thus, Nazi doctrine violates the fundamental values of Christianity and the West by creating a hierarchy of people from strong to weak, the latter including the elderly, the sick, and the unproductive. Far from being complicit in the Holocaust, Christians and conservatives fought against the euthanasia of the "useless" planned by the regime in the name of human dignity, a fight they won.[68] The Reich also rejected the Christian concept of marriage and fidelity, "a cultural artifact that cannot contradict natural decrees,"[69] which call for maximum reproduction, at the cost of dissolving sterile marriages and even permitting polygamy. In other words, Nazism cannot be placed in continuity with conservatism or Christianity, as historian Robert Paxton points out.[70] The Nazi project aimed to deliver the German race from its Judeo-Christian heritage, which it conceived as a curse. In Italy, Mussolini also presented his regime as a revolution, a "total transformation of Italy"[71] inspired by a military and warrior spirit. Joseph Goebbels, chief propagandist of the Reich, was determined to "bring down the old world and create a new one, to destroy to make way for a new creation, right to the last stone."[72] From this perspective, the failure of fascist regimes constitutes the failure of social engineering to reinvent human beings, the victory of tradition and culture over revolutionary totalitarianism. The goal of contemporary anti-fascism is quite different.

In fact, according to French geographer and essayist Christophe Guilluy, contemporary anti-fascist rhetoric is a "class weapon" that consists of denouncing as fascists those who publicly defend common people.[73] As pollster Jérôme Fourquet notes, there is now a strong correlation between level of education, place of residence, and attitude toward the nation and the "open society." The 54 percent of French people who have lived all or most of their lives in the same community therefore have a necessarily different relationship with the world of cosmopolitan university graduates, whose networks and friendships are much less concentrated and rooted in the same territory.[74] In his best-selling essay *The Road to Somewhere,*[75] British journalist David Goodhart also arrives at the same conclusion by theorizing the fault line between "Somewheres" and "Anywheres." However, this silent majority, whose priority is "the preservation of a protective social and cultural capital,"[76] is silenced in the open society, whose founding it threatens by reminding us that ordinary people still value the customs and traditions that shape their own sense of belonging.

By allowing itself to be convinced that the main culprits of the Holocaust were ordinary people, the culture of normality, and the ethic of duty, Western civilization has rebuilt its imagination against the figure of the majority. Whereas the common man was previously the reference point for community spirit and the nation-state, he is gradually made to look like Eichmann. The figure of the middle class, the ordinary man, and more generally the idea of normality gradually lose their prestige. Workers do not disappear from reality, but they are erased from culture and the media, losing "most of the status they had in collective representations."[77] Worse still, when they are mentioned, it is in terms of "an intrinsically racist and intellectually deficient population."[78] "*Petits blancs*" (little whites) in France, "chavs" in the United Kingdom, "white trash" and "deplorables" in the United States—there is no shortage of derogatory nicknames for those who were once at the heart of the democratic project. During the 2024 US election, President Joe Biden added "garbage" to the list of epithets used to describe populist voters. This has consequences for cultural integration: The average Americans and Europeans, now described as rednecks and racists, no longer have the social capital necessary for immigrants to want to join them and live like them. Who would want to become "trash" or "deplorable?" No one. As the common man is said to be nothing but prejudice and resentment, the prevailing view now advocates for the "liberation" from social and moral norms that are nevertheless indispensable to the social capital sustaining Western civilization.

CHAPTER 2

Freedom from Society

THE DECONSTRUCTION OF civilization that we have witnessed in the last fifty years has taken hold of the West in the name of freedom, a noble aspiration that has appealed to the human spirit throughout the ages. However, postwar political thought has stripped freedom of its positive and demanding content, which encouraged free subjects to surpass themselves in order to achieve an ideal of excellence higher than themselves. The misguided freedom that now prevails is that of the radical sixties—that of the famous May '68 slogan declaring "it is forbidden to forbid," a negative principle that attacks established norms. It has broken with the democratic ideal and defends the sovereignty of the individual against that of the people, instead of trying to reconcile the two. Behind its claim to neutrality and its promises of individual fulfillment, this new freedom promotes an escape from society and its obligations, which primarily benefits antisocial behavior, whereas the restrictive norms and laws of the past often served as safeguards against such excesses, to the benefit of a silent majority that suffers disproportionately from their dismantling.

Hell Is Other People

Fundamentally, freedom does not exist on its own. We are always free "from" something, and therefore "against" something. The contemporary interpretation of so-called "negative" freedom, theorized by Oxford philosopher Isaiah Berlin, is conceived as being against society rather than against the inner impulses that Kant mistrusted:

> The fundamental sense of freedom is freedom from chains, from imprisonment, from enslavement by others. The rest is extension of this sense, or else metaphor. To strive to be free is to seek to remove obstacles; to struggle for personal freedom is to seek to curb interference, exploitation, and enslavement by men whose ends are theirs, not one's own.[1]

Thus, this freedom is turned outward: it assumes that man is chained by others and must free himself, with no precise goal except the absence of constraint. In Mill's words, "All restraint, qua restraint, is an evil."[2] What vision of the common good do liberals pursue? What would their ideal society be? They generally do not claim to have one,[3] since they see man as infinitely perfectible. They see all individual desires as legitimate, as long as they do not interfere with those of others. This thinking resembles more a critical arsenal, fit to deconstruct but not to build. With the collapse of its positive ideals in the fallout of the totalitarian trauma, the West has embarked on "an eternal interim ethic of release from inherited controls."[4] This has given rise to a profound cynicism, which makes any positive project seem fraudulent or stupid in our eyes.[5] Unfortunately, this cynicism has moved beyond healthy mistrust of totalitarianism to intrude into the private sphere, making individual autonomy an absolute ideal, which new generations are fed from childhood:

> Autonomy is the one good in our culture that must not be compromised. Autonomy precludes being dependent on anyone. You are vulnerable if you rely on someone else. Trusting another person with your fate, leaning on someone, is weakness—it's a betrayal of your own self-determination. Independence and connection are often inversely related.[6]

With such a radical view of individuality, it is no surprise that social ties are now weaker than ever. French sociologist Geoffroy de Lagasnerie defends precisely this radical separation from others when he describes ideal humans as "rebellious, unruly beings who assert their radical independence from all institutions and rules, both external and internal, and manage to be their own foundation."[7] He dreams of an *à la carte* existence, a "self-foundational practice" that allows one to "distance oneself from sociable relationships that contribute nothing," in the face of a society that "appears as a whole to be an immense machine for standardization . . . subjecting everyone to an organization of life that does not respect the plurality of individual rhythms."[8] It would thus be a matter of fleeing "submission to sociability, and in particular its extreme form, which is family sociability,"[9] which is particularly troublesome for the autonomous individual. While the critique of the family explored in the previous chapter criticized it for its political consequences, namely that of fostering conservatism, this libertarian critique is even more radical: it criticizes the very nature of the family as a holistic and fundamentally non-individualistic institution, which escapes the logic of a contract that one can freely join or leave. By seeking to extend the sphere of autonomy to the family, there is a high risk of bringing about a veritable "disappearance of selflessness."[10]

It says a lot about our cultural moment that an individualistic critique of the family is gaining popularity in progressive spheres, particularly through the considerable attention recently given to the "No Kids" movement, young people who refuse to have children for ideological reasons. According to Lagasnerie, the family is nothing less than a "mechanism of existential dispossession" consisting of "having one's existence stolen by society and others."[11] Proof of this would be apparent in "the complaints expressed in the run-up to the holiday season, particularly on social media, about the anxiety of having to talk to that unpleasant relative or being woken up at 7 a.m. by the children the day after a party."[12] If these minor discomforts, which have always been part of human sociability, are now being challenged, it is because they are at odds with the spirit of the times, which calls instead for uncompromising satisfaction of our desires, even the most mundane ones. Feminist author Mona Chollet is wary of parenthood as an "injunction to forget oneself" and is glad that she "owes her time and energy to no one" rather than becoming "a mere auxiliary in the service of lives other than her own." She congratulates herself that "in my case, 'a little time for myself' is my whole life!"[13]

This unease expressed toward family life hides another, which targets any long-term commitment that limits personal freedom. "Leaving a relationship and family life is difficult when leaving a friendship is easy,"[14] which would justify mistrusting these strong bonds in favor of fleeting relationships that can be discarded at will. Similarly, the desire to have children appears to be "an attempt by the outside world to steal my conscience and my body," and buying a house ends up being a "trap," since it involves a long-term financial commitment.[15] This paranoid view of freedom, which fears commitment above all else, is evident today in the obsession with "keeping my options open," an expression that first appeared in the 1960s and has grown in popularity ever since.[16] If any meaningful commitment is to be avoided for fear of limiting our future possibilities, the ideal of a "free" life becomes solitude, emotional disengagement, and selfishness, in perpetual mistrust of others. This loss of trust in the community obviously has substantial consequences on a social level. The "fantasy" of libertarian critics of the family, by their own admission, is to "leave society" in order to find "a place outside society—a countercultural space where another way to live can be invented."[17]

The Fantasy of Leaving Society

This spirit of negation and mistrust toward what is common, which has been philosophically embodied on the left and right in anarchism and libertarianism, logically leads to the exit from society, the supreme proof of freedom. On the right, libertarianism seeks to defend individual freedom as a fundamental political norm, with the only limit being that of others.[18] Consequently, freedom becomes an article of faith and does not need to be justified in terms of any particular ends, especially not the common good, a notion they consider empty and vague. Libertarians conceive of politics as a struggle between two political camps, the only two that really exist in their eyes: freedom and coercion.[19] What connects them to the right is a reversed vision of class struggle, between those who produce wealth and those who steal it from them through the indirect means of taxation. Their defense of the individual is that of the strong against the weak, all mediocrities who wish to bring down to their level those who try to rise above them. This is the fantasy world Ayn Rand's novels: "Altruism . . . is a conspiracy perpetrated by the weak upon the strong, an attempt to handicap those whose natural superiority makes them a threat."[20] Consequently, morality has no place in politics, which should stick to establishing "a framework of rules that will guarantee each individual the freedom to pursue his own good in his own way."[21] The atomistic perspective of libertarians makes them extremely skeptical of state power, and even of its monopoly on legitimate violence.[22] If the state is not particularly legitimate, neither is the nation, unless it has obtained the individual consent of each individual to be a member, ignoring the cultural nature of the development of nations. This argument was formulated by Lysander Spooner at the time of the American Civil War, in his pamphlet *No Treason*:

> How do millions of such men come to be a nation, in the first place? How is it that each of them comes to be stripped of his natural, God-given rights, and to be incorporated, compressed, compacted, and consolidated into a mass with other men, whom he never saw; with whom he has no contract; and towards many of whom he has no sentiments but fear, hatred, or contempt?[23]

This antisocial sensibility finds its left-wing counterpart in anarchism, whose imaginary is also that of "a single man who insists on being free" against "a multitude of silent slaves."[24] It is therefore not a democratic sensibility, as it prefers the sovereignty of the individual to the sovereignty of the people.[25] Here again, the state is a system of domination,[26] but instead of being a tool of the weak against the strong, it is said to alienate good men by forcing them into competition with their peers. For the anarchist thinker Peter Kropotkin, the end of the repression of crimes would in itself bring about the end of crime, a naive prospect if ever there was one: "Leave men absolutely free. Do not mutilate them as religions have done enough and to spare. Do not fear even their passions. In a free society these are not dangerous."[27] Anarchism thus offers a left-wing version of the invisible hand doctrine, according to which the pursuit of private interest is a public virtue:

> In general, the moralists who built their systems on an alleged opposition between egoist sentiments and altruist sentiments have taken the wrong path. If this opposition existed in reality, if the good of the individual was really opposed to that of society, the human race would not exist . . . there is always found, in the animal world as in the human race, a large number of individuals who did not understand that the good of the individual and that of the species are, at bottom, identical. They did not understand that to live an intense life is the purpose of every individual, he finds the greatest intensity of life in the greatest sociability, in the most perfect identification of himself with all those around him.[28]

In their criticism of social control, anarchists also reject the concept of morality: "the more we undermine the foundations of the established morality, or rather of the hypocrisy that takes its place—the more the moral level of society is raised."[29] Anarchism, eschewing notions of good and evil, recognizes only pleasure as the ultimate aim of the individual, which does not make it any different from libertarianism or liberalism. It seems that the twin doctrines of libertarianism and anarchism actually converge in nihilism, a way of thinking "that bows to no authority, that makes no principle an article of faith, no matter how much respect that principle is surrounded by," "a way of thinking without foundation(s), radically negative, which, beyond doubt, proclaims with constancy and despair a rejection of everything, an adherence to nothing."[30]

This is no accident. The logical outcome of libertarianism and anarchism, and consequently of liberalism, which, according to Berlin, is only a watered-down version of this creed,[31] is the abandonment of the social contract, whose contractual nature they take at face value. Libertarian thinker Robert Nozick argues that it should be possible for all citizens to opt out of the welfare state, and thus of both taxation and social services.[32] In other words, people should not have to emigrate to leave their country's social system and the obligations it imposes on them. Anarchist activists, for their part, advocate the establishment of "autonomous zones,"[33] areas of lawlessness where law enforcement no longer has jurisdiction and where individuals would achieve absolute autonomy. Anarchism and libertarianism both challenge the universality of citizens' subjection to laws. They share the same ideal of leaving the community, expressed in different words.

For Lysander Spooner, a man subject to a government he does not want is a slave, just as much as one who works in a cotton field, give or take a few degrees.[34] Rejecting a society or nation that one has not chosen oneself cannot be considered treason, because no formal commitment was ever made in the first place.[35] Moreover, it would be impossible to consent to it voluntarily: "there is not the slightest probability that there is a single man in the country, who both understands what the Constitution really is, and sincerely supports it for what it really is,"[36] because it would be a tool used by a minority of rulers to seize power with the support of an unconscious majority. This is a paradox of freedom as envisioned by liberals: the only way to be free, according to Spooner, is to abandon the Constitution, because to support it in full knowledge of the facts would be impossible except for a subhuman who does not make full use of his freedom. The borderless left comes to much the same conclusion by asserting that, far from conferring rights on human beings, the principle of citizenship makes them the property of the state, which is then free to use violence against them.[37] Moreover, it would fundamentally be a structure of "exclusion" by drawing a line between citizens and non-citizens. The only solution to avoid exclusion would be to abolish the principle of citizenship and borders along with it. Unlike Nozick, who wanted the rich to have the right to opt out of the taxation and social protection system, borderlessness demands the right for all humans on Earth to benefit from the welfare state, without necessarily contributing to it.[38] In both cases, there is a breach of the duty of reciprocity that binds citizens within a democratic state: individual sovereignty serves antisocial behaviors and violates the social norms that uphold the common good. Is this narcissistic individual, in perpetual avoidance of their obligations, really as happy as libertarian doctrine would have us believe?

Escape from Duty and Escape from Reality

The repercussions of the sixties give us a glimpse of what the individual shaped by freedom looks like in practice, once turned against society. First, we see a rehabilitation of narcissism, anticipated by Christopher Lasch in *The Culture of Narcissism* and championed by self-help philosophers such as Fabrice Midal. Midal reinterprets the myth of Narcissus, portraying the handsome Greek hunter not as a vain man excessively in love with himself, but as an insecure character who was unaware of his own beauty before "encountering himself."[39] In line with the prevailing individualistic discourse, he appropriates the cliché that "everyone is special," a contradiction in itself that allows everyone to become an outsider in their own way, to leave the majority behind and assert their difference: "We are all ugly little ducklings destined to become swans—if we want to."[40] Under the slogan "become what you are,"[41] self-help ironically does not invite us to step outside ourselves, but rather to dive deep inside to take refuge there, because everything we need could be found within ourselves. Obviously, if we are already perfect, there is no point in improving. The philosophy of "letting go" invites us to love ourselves as we are rather than aim higher and to stop the "permanent war against ourselves"[42] inherent in Kantian duty. Mona Chollet denounces self-criticism as an "inner enemy," which is "nothing more than the result of the long sedimentation, within us, of an external enemy," a "layer of hatred" produced by a "deleterious culture" inherited from Christianity.[43] To remedy this, she invites us to avoid self-questioning and to embrace the figure of the snowflake, long derided by conservatives as the caricature of a generation where everyone believes themselves to be special.[44] Rather than striving to become someone else, more knowledgeable or better, the goal of education thus becomes "the learning of imperfection,"[45] or accepting mediocrity. Above all, it is about protecting one's individuality from anything higher than oneself: "The dominant political, economic, and moral discourse in our so-called democratic societies still asks us, as Stalin and Hitler did, to sacrifice ourselves for the collective, the common good—of the system, the group, the family, the company."[46] Individuality would be the highest authority, because we would all be brilliant in our own way. Being attentive to the needs of others, and even more so sacrificing some part of our happiness for them, would be an obstacle to the sovereignty of the individual.

Should we be surprised by the explosion of self-esteem over the last fifty years? In the 1950s, only 12 percent of American teenagers said they were "an important person," a statement that seemed arrogant to them; by the early 1980s, that proportion had risen to 80 percent.[47] From the paradox of everyone being special, psychologist Jean M. Twenge theorizes the rise of "empty" self-esteem, a form of self-esteem that is unrelated to any significant achievement.[48] Believing that "I am special simply because I am me," and not because I am exceptional or successful in one area or another, can even prove perverse, in that I will not want to work harder to improve myself.

Since the revolution of the 1960s, mental health has also become a major social issue, and the trend has accelerated considerably in recent years. Depression and distress have increased, and what Anne Case and Angus Deaton call "deaths of despair,"[49] such as suicides and overdoses, have skyrocketed.[50] British psychologist Theodore Dalrymple sees this as a contemporary inability to accept the tragic dimension of existence, whether it be the fact of being average (which is nothing to be ashamed of) or being dissatisfied, a perpetual condition of the human soul.[51] Individuals who believe themselves to be sovereign find it harder than ever to come to terms with the limitations imposed on them by nature, which they can never escape. The more they focus on themselves, the more unhappy they become. Peter Singer describes the "paradox of hedonism," according to which those who seek happiness do not find it, but those who do not explicitly seek it find it by devoting themselves to goals and causes that transcend them.[52]

The motto "YOLO"—you only live once—is symptomatic of the replacement of the ethics of duty with utilitarianism, which asserts that "pleasure, and freedom from pain, are the only things desirable as ends."[53] The implication is that the old norms made people unhappy by subjecting them to all kinds of obligations and "ideologies based on the postponement of gratification."[54] Thus, these new principles have changed the meaning of institutions such as marriage, which is no longer an institution of cooperation and reproduction of the social order, and work, which is no longer primarily a means of earning a living. Both are now at the service of individual pleasure and detached from their share of responsibility, hence the rise of "polyamory" and the "dream job" of influencer among teenagers. For Kant, "letting one's potential rust" was a failure to fulfill one's duty to oneself to develop fully, as well as a fault toward others. Even Karl Marx saw work as "an eternal necessity, an indispensable mediation in the metabolism that occurs between man and nature, and therefore indispensable to human life."[55] Now, a majority of French people are in favor of the idea of "working less to earn less," the opposite of Nicolas Sarkozy's famous slogan in 2007, "work more to earn more."[56] Green politician Sandrine

Rousseau praises the "right to laziness," while Mona Chollet defends "resistance through resting" to protest against the "imperative of productivity."[57] As Raymond Aron sensed, individuals now demand everything from society but give nothing back.[58]

What if reality was no longer sufficient to attain pleasure? Philosopher Luc Ferry fears the advent of the "metaverse," an immersive and realistic virtual world that would allow a decisive escape from reality rather than postponing happiness in a real world that, although freed from substantial duties, remains subject to natural constraints.[59] In a way, Robert Nozick had already anticipated this with his theory of the "experience machine," asking whether a life connected to a machine that makes us happy, as in *The Matrix*, would really be superior to a real existence. He concludes that "plugging into the machine is a kind of suicide,"[60] because authentic life cannot be reduced to purely subjective sensations. On the contrary, contact with others and the real world is inseparable from the human experience, despite the frustrations it may cause. Nevertheless, the distorted existence offered by the machine would be the most perfect version of individual sovereignty, finally freed from natural constraints in a virtual world subject to its desires. But this life would not be human, just like the desire to leave society, which lies at the heart of the libertarian ideal.

Without the metaverse to flee civilization, at least for now, Jean-Jacques Rousseau's fantasy of returning to an idealized state of nature remains a powerful illusion. Christopher Ryan's best-selling book *Civilized to Death* can be read as a contemporary update of *Discourse on the Origin and Basis of Inequality Among Men* and takes up its vision of an individual who is freer than ever from social constraints. Thus, the ascetic idea that one must work to achieve happiness and dilute one's pleasure stems from an overspecialized society that has dissociated vital needs by outsourcing the enjoyable activities practiced by our ancestors, the noble savages, such as hunting and fishing.[61] Similarly, ambition would be unhealthy and detrimental to happiness, like most of the demands constructed by civilization. According to Ryan, humanity has gone "from living in the world to living in a zoo of its own making,"[62] whose laws, norms, and customs require behavior that is often in direct conflict with human nature and the instincts that have been ours for millennia. However, by encouraging everyone to follow their impulses and disregard customs, libertarian ethics have led to oppression far worse than civilization's salutary restrictions on human impulses.

Free to Be Violent?

In recent years, the rise of social and cultural issues in politics has led to a political divide that no longer pits the left against the right on economic matters, but rather the friends and enemies of coercion. This very concept, which has become unfashionable in "open" society as it is synonymous with rigidity and closed-mindedness, is discredited even when it is eminently necessary for the well-being of the most vulnerable. For the libertarian left, drug use is therefore becoming a "perfectly rational and sometimes empowering response to current social and political conditions," the prohibition of which would disconnect individuals from their bodies and their own feelings.[63] The application of anti-coercive ideas, particularly on the North American west coast, reveals the devastation of this logic when applied in practice.

In the Canadian province of British Columbia, the progressive government of Premier David Eby had decided to decriminalize the possession of hard drugs such as fentanyl, cocaine, and MDMA for personal use. Far from having the expected positive effects, which would result from less "stigmatization" of addicts, this policy has led to a drastic increase in the open use of hard drugs in parks, public transportation, and hospitals.[64] In addition to preventing police from intervening to protect the public, "decriminalization reduces prices by lowering production and distribution costs [for dealers], which increases use."[65] In the wake of this, the provincial government of British Columbia set up a "*safer supply*" program for hard drugs for drug addicts. With "harm reduction" in mind, the state began distributing so-called "safer" opioids for free on the streets, with the predictable result that dealers appropriated them for resale, thereby expanding their business model at no cost. By distributing 11 million tablets of hydromorphone, an opioid as powerful as heroin, the government of British Columbia, far from reducing drug-related harm, increased the amount in circulation in its territory by a third.[66] The effect of these policies was so damaging to Vancouver residents that barely a year after their introduction, Premier David Eby had no choice but to backtrack and publicly acknowledge the liberalization of hard drugs as a failure.

A little further south, San Francisco is grappling with the same addiction epidemic, and the same libertarian resistance to a coercive response to the opioid crisis. In this ultra-progressive city, the involuntary treatment of drug addicts, who often suffer from mental illness and pose a threat to their own safety and that of others, is controversial: in the name of the "inalienable" right to refuse medical treatment, dangerous individuals are left free because they wish to remain so. The predictable consequence of this policy was the murder in 2001 of three people, including Laura Wilcox, a nineteen-year-old student, by a man suffering from paranoia and agoraphobia who had refused treatment. This tragedy led to the adoption of "Laura's Law," which allows for the involuntary hospitalization of dangerous patients. Nevertheless, the principle of the law remains controversial, particularly among activists who seem "more interested in people's civil rights than in their lives."[67] When it comes to drug addiction, there is a fundamental conflict between absolute freedom and public safety, yet many take the side of the former over the latter, with dramatic consequences.

The libertarian view of the police and criminal justice is just as dangerous. According to activists who want to "defund the police," cracking down on crime "merely creates new victims,"[68] as new people would be subjected to state coercion without real redress. Thus, punishing criminals for their misdeeds would not be justice, but rather a reproduction of the violence that the criminal justice system claims to combat. Québécois law professor and columnist Aurélie Lanctôt therefore advocates the abolition of prisons to avoid "responding to violence with violence,"[69] in the naive belief that the fight against poverty would be enough to curb criminal activity. However, when the police do not play their role in violent contexts, ordinary citizens suffer the consequences. For example, the riots that took place in Minnesota in 2020 in the name of the Black Lives Matter (BLM) movement severely affected small business owners in Minneapolis, such as African American entrepreneur Chris Montana, owner of a distillery. Rioters set fires in several places in his shop, stole his alcohol inventory, and triggered the store's sprinklers, which flooded the premises and caused considerable property damage.[70] This violence, committed in the name of social progress and the African American cause by anti-police activists, has direct negative consequences for the groups it claims to protect. It is clear that Chris Montana would have preferred the police to intervene to save his business, rather than see it ravaged by rioters in the name of "social justice."

The failure of this philosophy was exposed once again when activists affiliated with the BLM movement set up an "autonomous zone" in the Capitol Hill neighborhood. The city of Seattle ordered the police to withdraw from the neighborhood, creating a truly lawless zone. Predictably, the most heavily armed rascals took control. Robberies, rapes, and even the murders of two black men took place in the name of anti-racism and liberation from police oppression, before law enforcement broke up the insurrection almost a month later.[71] This experience brings to mind fundamental observations that date back to Hobbes' *Leviathan*: "What protects us from violence is that we all know that the state can exercise the violence we have delegated to it."[72] Pure negative freedom resembles the film series *The Purge*, in which the state suspends its role for twenty-four hours and makes all crimes legal, including murder. No one benefits from the criminal justice system being truly abolished, lest we fall into the "war of all against all" that the modern state has rightly helped to contain. To backtrack on this fundamental achievement of civilization would lower us to constant fear and the danger of violent death that makes human life "nasty, brutish, and short," in Hobbes' famous words. Conversely, the anti-justice and anti-police stance in vogue today is as absurd as that of philosopher Bertrand Russell, who advocated for the disarmament of England during World War II: "If Chancellor Adolf Hitler and his troops ever invade Britain they should be welcomed like tourists and greeted in a friendly way . . . The Nazis would find some interest in our way of living, I think, and the starch would be taken out of them."[73] Fortunately, Winston Churchill did not take his arguments seriously at the time, or the "free world" would no longer be free today.

"Free" Love and Its Discontents

Sexuality is certainly the area where freedom has been most touted over the past fifty years. Finally freed from the malicious tutelage of religion, men and (especially) women would finally be free to indulge their sensual impulses! However, the #MeToo movement, which shook the world in 2017, revealed the excesses of absolute sexual freedom, which gives free rein to power games that systematically inferiorize women. Louise Perry, in *The Case Against the Sexual*

Revolution, makes a provocative observation: the real winners of the sexual revolution are actually Hugh Hefner, founder of *Playboy*, and all the rich and powerful men who gained access to numerous women whom they were able to exploit at will.

The prism of freedom tends to erase the differences between men and women: everyone is imagined as equal in terms of their needs, resources, and physical strength. However, this ignores the fundamental asymmetries in heterosexuality;[74] while men tend to seek out more different partners and more fleeting relationships, women on average seek more stability and a long-term investment in an emotional relationship.[75] We can guess the biological imperatives behind these disparities: It is perfectly normal for women, who can become pregnant, to want a long-term relationship in which the man is committed and participates in family life. As in the economic sphere, total freedom therefore creates winners and losers, because behind laissez-faire there are power relations. In this case, men can still afford to have more relationships than women, despite widespread use of contraception. More specifically, sexual laissez-faire directly benefits people who are unromantic and non-monogamous, who want to have multiple conquests, something that the "old moral order" repressed. Conversely, monogamous people who seek long-term relationships are at a distinct disadvantage, as they feel that the new libertarian norm makes them exceptions, if not oddballs. This creates "a sense of obligation, that is, an internalized normalization of practices that were once marginal," which means that "yes is the default and no is more difficult to say,"[76] because young women feel the pressure not to be "prudish" or come across as teasing. In a competitive market such as that of romantic relationships, not conforming to the norm comes at a cost, and it is now the less libertine who pay the price:

> If I am, for instance, a young female student looking for a boyfriend at my twenty-first-century university, and I don't

> want to have sex before marriage, then I will find my options limited in a way that they wouldn't have been seventy years ago. When sex before marriage is expected, and when almost all of the other women participating in my particular sexual market are willing to "put out" on a first or second date, then not being willing to do the same becomes a competitive disadvantage.[77]

Defenders of negative freedom fail to point out that the tyranny of the majority exists just as much, if not more, in a "free" context than under the rule of a norm designed to be fair and just. Or perhaps they were well aware of this: many icons of sixties radicalism, Michel Foucault, in particular, spoke out in favor of lowering the age of sexual consent, thus clearly prioritizing the freedom of the strong (adults) over that of the weak (children).

Similarly, libertines argue that the criminalization of prostitution is a "form of state moralism that is difficult to accept in a secular and pluralistic democracy, since it seeks to dictate to citizens the best way to have sex (free rather than paid)."[78] The principle of non-commodification of the body has no intrinsic value for them, representing instead "prejudices linked to our culture, 'conventions' specific to our societies, which are neither eternal nor universal." A truly free humanity, argues philosopher Ruwen Ogien, would make peace with its body and consider its parts "no longer as quasi-sacred things that constitute our identity, but as objects as replaceable as a kitchen table or a washing machine."[79] Selling sexual favors would become a dangerous job, certainly, but neither immoral nor degrading for those who practice it, much like deep-sea fishing or mixed martial arts. The figure of the prostitute would thus be the freest woman imaginable, a man-eater with no attachments or children, and cultural representations of the "liberated woman" often come close to this. However, as philosopher Camille Dejardin points out, this archetype "embodies a part of male desires far more than it emancipates itself from them."[80] Producer Harvey Weinstein, for example, was formally convicted of rape, but he also offered roles to young actresses in exchange for consensual sexual relations. If sex is a service like any other and "sex work is work," this kind of behavior would have been celebrated. However, this exchange of favors has rightly aroused the ire of the entire feminist movement—even those on the fringes who advocate for the legalization of prostitution. It certainly betrays a form of hypocrisy, which hides inequalities not only between the sexes, but also and above all between classes. How come what is said to be a free choice, when poor or drug-addicted women sell their bodies to a pimp, becomes despicable when the same act happens in the affluent world of Hollywood?

Sadomasochism reveals a similar short-sightedness of the ethics of freedom when it comes to inequalities resulting from laissez-faire. The individuals who participate in it appear independent and rational, but the unequal dynamic is revealed when, "in the vast majority of cases, BDSM practices occur between one or more dominant men and one or more submissive women."[81] Insofar as all desires are valid, and men must listen to their impulses, even the most harmful ones, they are perfectly free to claim this "freedom to hurt, degrade, and humiliate"[82] women through sadomasochism. Curiously, what would be considered a crime in any other context, such as assault or domestic violence, becomes legitimate when it takes place in the bedroom. The same violent act would be criminal or not depending on the victim (girlfriend or not) and their disposition at the time (consenting or not).

Ruwen Ogien points out that the libertarian logic of consent reaches its limits with these examples, in the sense that those who attempt to restrict prostitution or BDSM while remaining strictly orthodox in their belief in individual choice enter into a contradictory line of reasoning that does not admit moral values, but still maintains that it would be impossible to fully consent to certain things.[83] Many progressives proclaim that consent should be the sole criterion in all things, but change their minds when they see the tangible results of their prescription, including flagrant violations of human dignity. These examples remind us that freely consented choice, while always necessary, is sometimes insufficient to justify practices that are obviously immoral and objectively harmful to others. Prioritizing the expression of men's violent impulses against women through BDSM rather than their suppression through self-control is a dangerous game.

Relativists who place different "family models" on an equal footing, claiming that a lasting relationship under the same roof is in no way preferable to single parenthood or polyamory, also disregard the well-being of the most vulnerable, namely children. Sociologist Brad Wilcox of the University of Virginia reveals, on the contrary, that family stability is one of the most important predictors of a child's future life. Young adults from intact families are twice as likely to obtain a university degree as those from separated families, and the latter are twice as likely to have behavioral problems at school, regardless of their income level. Depression is also 50 percent more common among children from unstable families. Surprisingly, the 1997 National Longitudinal Study of Youth even shows that young American men who grow up in single-parent families are more likely to go to prison (21 percent) than to obtain a university degree (14 percent).[84] The point is not to deny that it is better to raise a child alone than with an abusive or violent partner, but to realize that freedom for some most often comes at a cost to others. The weakening of families in recent decades has led to greater instability than in the past, and it is children who have suffered the consequences. The divorce rate in the United States has fallen since the 1980s, partly because many children of divorce do not want to inflict this pain on their own children.[85]

Norms Protect the Weak

The problem of negative freedom as a totalizing ethic can be summed up in a paradox. In *The Open Society and Its Enemies*, Karl Popper argues that the fundamental question of politics should not be "who should rule?" in the sense of what vision of the good to pursue, but rather "how can we organize political institutions so that bad or incompetent rulers can be prevented from doing too much damage?"[86] The view of liberals, who are supremely distrustful of state action, only considers the tyranny of the public and never warns of private tyranny. In *Tyranny Inc* journalist Sohrab Ahmari reminds us that "coercion is far more widespread in supposedly noncoercive societies than we would like to think—provided we pay attention to private power and admit the possibility of *private coercion*."[87] In this regard, the notion of consent is not a good in itself, but often a fig leaf covering up "the sheer power of private individuals and entities to coerce us as consumers, workers, and citizens."[88] Nevertheless, the Poppers of this world believe they can avoid evil by preventing the state from defending a vision of good . . . and at the same time granting the powerful the right to do as they please under the guise of freedom.

Like laws, customs are cultural boundaries that prevent antisocial behavior. This is a lesson that the left understood before taking the libertarian turn and that the right is reappropriating today, because it is as true, if not more so, in the social sphere as it is in the economic sphere: "We are rediscovering that freedom does not exist in the absence of constraints, because it quickly becomes submission to the law of the strongest, and that it can only flourish within moral law."[89] Moreover, the conception of norms and laws as a form of "tyranny of the majority" needs to be reevaluated. In libertarian discourse, they oppress the sovereign individual, but it is omitted that they also protect society from the strong and the malicious, who tend to take advantage of an overly lax framework. Far from being tyrannical, they are profoundly democratic, since they have been refined through generations of lived experience, but above all because they protect the fulfillment of each individual, regardless of their strength or economic position.[90] The ethics of duty, which we now equate with alienation, forced the elites and the powerful to take the collective interest into consideration and to regulate their own actions, something they no longer have to do when their guiding principle becomes you only live once.

Against utopian claims that social constraints are the cause of the excesses they seek to limit, let us remember with Chesterton that "original sin [is] almost the first thing to be believed in," because "a permanent possibility of selfishness arises from the mere fact of having a self."[91] This is the most important lesson of all great religions, which retains its value even in a largely secularized civilization. Harvard psychologist Steven Pinker, in his book *The Blank Slate*, demonstrates that violence and antisocial behavior are natural and not cultural. For example, 90 percent of hunter-gatherer societies practiced warfare, and two-thirds were at war at least once every two years.[92] Similarly, toddlers are statistically the most violent age group,[93] and society civilizes them so that they learn to repress this violence, rather than become mean by becoming sociable, as Rousseau would say. Statistics on rape show the same pattern: young men in their twenties are disproportionately guilty of it, and the frequency drops dramatically with age.[94] If young people are indeed "conditioned" by "rape culture," as we sometimes hear, what "deconditions" them so that, after the age of thirty, this urge fades away? It is culture and norms that signal to individuals that there will be a social price to pay for those who harm others.

The Freedom of the Selfish Rebel

In the eyes of the ethics of duty, the now dominant view of individuality resembles what Richard Dawkins, author of *The Selfish Gene*, calls the "selfish rebel, prepared to exploit the altruism of the rest."[95] In morality, as in economics, there are net contributors and net debtors, because common goods such as security, a shared culture, and social capital depend on the efforts of a silent majority, which curbs its antisocial impulses for the good of the whole.[96] Too often, those who claim freedom rely on the fact that morality applies to others, but not to them: they want to escape general constraints without the disadvantages they would suffer if everyone did the same. In other words, the freedom of a few "selfish rebels" depends on the contribution of a conformist majority that does not enjoy the same privilege, since it provides the framework that makes this freedom possible: "One wonders to what extent the barring of individuality to many is the *sine qua non* of the individuality of some; whether individuality, in its present rendition, can be anything other than a privilege."[97] The enjoyment of the Marquis de Sade and Hugh Hefner thus required the inferiorization of women less fortunate than themselves. Most of the examples cited in this chapter reproduce this pattern, whereby a libertine minority benefits from the social capital generated by the discipline of others. Their behavior is based on the fact that others will not act as they do, and it would not pass the test of universality by which Kant judges the morality of an action.

Worse still, many of these morally liberal positions correspond to what American psychologist Rob Henderson calls "luxury beliefs," or "ideas and opinions that confer upper-class status at very little cost, while often inflicting costs on the lower classes."[98] Thus, in order to appear open-minded, intellectuals and bourgeois may support dangerous ideas such as the abolition of the police, the decriminalization of all drugs, the legalization of prostitution, polyamory, and the devaluation of marriage . . . because they will never experience the consequences themselves. It is working-class neighborhoods that are most affected by crime, violence, drug addiction, and family instability, which is precisely why people from the middle and lower classes are more culturally conservative than the economic elites, who take for granted the stability and security that social capital provides.

Today, are "moral order" and public coercion really still the two beasts against which freedom must be defined? Philosopher Matthew B. Crawford argues that, on the contrary, "the everyday threats to your well-being no longer come from an ideological rival or a theological threat to the liberal secular order. They are native to that order."[99] The mistake of the libertarian ideal was to make people believe that they live in a world that they are free to rewrite as they please, and individuality has thus acquired a form of primacy over culture, norms, and even, more recently, biology, since the chosen gender has replaced the sex "assigned at birth." Yet the world is not our creation, and evolving in a context that pre-exists us is a fundamental part of the human experience, marked by determinisms of our physical existence, our nature as social animals, and the historical moment in which we live.[100] If we lose sight of these factors that inevitably affect our freedom, we sink into a narcissism that does not make us more independent but, on the contrary, more vulnerable. It mobilizes the energies of the individual against the "tyrannies of the public," but leaves us vulnerable to those energies that operate outside the sphere of the state, and especially to those energies that lie dormant within ourselves. However, in order to shape the world in one's own image, one must accept and understand one's rootedness, like the craftsman or musician, who can only exercise his creativity through patient and sincere submission to an established tradition, in which he inscribes his art and his freedom.[101] This "demanding" individualism, which leads to true freedom, has been replaced by a complacent individualism that deprives man of his true independence and pits him against society. Far from being self-evident, negative freedom carries within it an antisocial drift, the logical end of which is the reign of the strong over the weak—a predatory individuality alien to society.

CHAPTER 3

How Authenticity Undermines the Common Good

ALTHOUGH NEGATIVE FREEDOM APPEARS to be a neutral concept, which does not convey any particular worldview and offers everyone the freedom to choose, the picture is more complex. By seeking to counter the "tyranny of custom," it has fueled a desire for differentiation and a counterculture that seeks to institutionalize dissent against the "disciplinary society." In this representation, most famously theorized by Michel Foucault, eccentricity is intrinsically superior to the norm, since it brings emancipation in the face of oppressive uniformity, and therefore deserves to be defended for its own sake against established customs. Nonconformity thus proves to be just as normative as the order it patiently deconstructs. The difference is that this new, culturally dominant paradigm stirs up identity-based conflicts rather than appeasing them by weakening the unifying rules that enable citizens to live together in a democracy.

The Self against the World

The prevailing mindset since the 1960s has been that of counterculture, or the elevation of subversion and rebellion as supreme values. Since Eichmann allegedly committed radical evil through fulfillment of duty, a simulacrum of perpetual "resistance" appears to many as an antidote to civilization's guilty conscience. Joseph Heath and Andrew Potter, in *The Rebel Sell*, summarize the promise of counterculture:

> What people need to be liberated from is not a specific class that oppresses them or a system of exploitation that imposes poverty upon them. People have become trapped in a gilded cage, and have been taught to love their own enslavement. "Society" controls them by limiting the imagination and suppressing their deepest needs. What they need is to escape from conformity. And to do so, they must reject the culture in its entirety. They must form a counterculture—one based on freedom and individuality.[1]

This creed goes beyond the mere freedom of the individual, which it instrumentalizes in the service of a normative program. Unlike many revolutionary movements of the past, counterculture does not (openly) seek to replace one regime with another, to substitute a new, positive horizon for the old one. It is not current institutions that pose a problem, but rather the existence of institutions and collective norms designed to regulate relations between people. Because totalitarian regimes have coerced citizens to do evil in the past, coercion itself should be abolished. In the words of Québécois sociologist Mathieu Bock-Côté, counterculture seeks to "reveal, through the socialization processes provided by traditional institutions, a general dynamic of alienation:"[2] law-abiding citizens and ordinary people should break free from their submission by subverting social codes as a way to free themselves from the heavy burden of norms weighing on them.

The countercultural mindset is an imaginary construct of alienation, whose most important thinker is undoubtedly Foucault. The "disciplinary society"[3] he describes in his works represents a malignant and elusive force, hanging like a sword of Damocles over the heads of individuals, particularly eccentrics and those who contradict established norms. He takes inspiration from the famous theory of panopticism, based on the prison designed by Jeremy Bentham, where convicts feel they are being watched at all times:

> The panoptic schema, without disappearing as such or losing any of its properties, was destined to spread throughout the social body; its vocation was to become a generalized function . . . Panopticism is the general principle of a new "political anatomy" whose object and end are not the relations of sovereignty but the relations of discipline.[4]

In this dystopian reading of reality, "all those systems of micro-power that are essentially non-egalitarian and asymmetrical that we call the disciplines"[5] form the invisible foundation of law and encourage conformity. Prison becomes the revealer of human existence, and every institution is a watered-down version of it, just as every law-abiding citizen is a potential Eichmann: "Is it surprising that prisons resemble factories, schools, barracks, hospitals, which all resemble prisons?"[6] Like Adorno and Reich before him, Foucault describes society as it is in pejorative terms: social contract thinkers, particularly Hobbes and Locke, advocate entry into society based on the coercion of individual wills. Why leave the state of nature, if not to protect oneself from arbitrariness and the law of the strongest, within a rational order based on the monopoly of violence? Foucault's critique thus runs counter to the founding principles of modern democratic revolutions.

Laws are also criticized in their claim to universality. Rather than ensuring the common good, they are depicted as a tool in a "class struggle" between conformists and dissidents: "[I]n the courts society as a whole does not judge one of its members, but that a social category with an interest in order judges another that is dedicated to disorder."[7] In countercultural thinking, the struggle between the proletariat and the bourgeoisie is relegated to the background, behind the question of coercion: it is the constrained against the constraining, the restricted against the restrictive. This new class struggle is also, inevitably, that of the "normal" against the "abnormal":

> Accustomed to using our own (genuine or putative) traits as the yardstick by which the humanity of other people is measured and assessed, we—the "normals"—"believe the person with a stigma is not quite human." The direct outcome of all that is a blunt refusal of social acceptance and a forceful alienation of people branded as anomalous.[8]

Cultural norms are now seen to be just as problematic as the laws they inspire, because they are conceived by and for the "normal," the common man, who, let us remember, was at the heart of the democratic ideal until very recently. Foucault therefore recommends insubordination, asserting that "crime constitutes a political instrument that could prove as precious for the liberation of our society as it has been for the emancipation of the Negroes."[9] Since conformity itself appears suspect, human greatness becomes the preserve of a dissident minority, oppressed throughout history by disciplinary society. This polarization between rebels and conformists classifies everyone into one camp or the other and leads to the glorification of madness in Foucault's writing. "Crazy people are not really crazy, they're just different. They aren't sick, they're non-conformists, drugged up and incarcerated to prevent them from asking too many difficult questions."[10] Consequently, the countercultural prism outlines what it considers to be the free, true individual: It is that which remains, against all odds, "authentic" in the face of the disciplinary society's demands for conformity.

Authenticity in the "Society of Identities"

If society really is a permanent assault on individuals, the latter have no choice but to differentiate themselves vigorously from the authoritarian mass that seeks to engulf them, never to "confuse what we are with what society has made of us."[11] Kantian morality, along with its Christian and Greek antecedents, according to which man is divided between good and evil and should be wary of his excessive impulses, thus becomes an authoritarian doctrine, since it curbs the self and forces it to seek a compromise with the outside. It is replaced by "expressive individualism," a term coined by sociologist Robert Bellah, according to which "each person has a unique core of feeling and intuition that should unfold or be expressed if individuality is to be realized."[12] In other words, it is now our responsibility to express our individual inner lives rather than consider ourselves as integrated into communities bound by natural or transcendent laws. This is, in fact, a normative reversal: since reason has become alienation, only impulses are authentic. The contradiction between certain personal desires or particularities and society, once normal, becomes hypocrisy. Expressive individualism is an ethic of authenticity, like the one Charles Taylor describes in his famous text on the "politics of recognition":

> There is a certain way of being human that is my way. I am called upon to live my life in this way, and not in imitation of

> anyone else's life. But this notion gives a new importance to being true to myself. If I am not, I miss the point of my life; I miss what being human is for me . . . Not only should I not mold my life to the demands of external conformity; I can't even find the model by which to live outside myself. I can only find it within.[13]

This vision of authenticity has collective consequences, according to which failure to recognize perceived identity can "inflict harm, can be a form of oppression, imprisoning someone in a false, distorted, and reduced mode of being."[14] The necessary distinction between a person and the way they act is abolished, and "any attempt to express disapproval is therefore a blow not simply against particular ways of behaving, but against the right of that person to be whoever they wish to be."[15]

The "society of individuals" is effectively shifting toward a "society of identities,"[16] where identity groups multiply as autonomous subjects of law, which can take legal action to invalidate laws that would cause them particular harm. According to the eminent American legal philosopher Ronald Dworkin, rights are "trumps,"[17] since they take precedence over collective objectives, just as in card games, trumps take precedence over other suits. Those who belong to a "protected group" under charters and bills of rights can therefore use them to ensure that their will takes precedence over that of the polity as a whole, unlike ordinary people, whom American essayist Jeremy Carl rightly describes as the "unprotected class."[18] This is, in a way, the *à la carte* existence that countercultural theorists dreamed of, in the form of a privilege restricted to those who can claim "authenticity" in our era. The "normal" people, for their part, cannot do much to resist this deconstruction from below.

The work of Judith Butler, gender ideology's leading theorist, is directly in line with this radical critique of normativity. While most people understand that there is a difference between gender as a product of culture and sex as an objective biological reality, she takes issue with this now "conservative" interpretation. In *Who's Afraid of Gender?* she asserts that biological sex does not exist, but is rather an arbitrary categorization system assigned by "medical and legal authorities" at birth.[19] Being born male or female is not an objective reality, but a normative system that "also communicates a set of adult desires and expectations"[20] as a form of violence against the authenticity of each individual, which is thus forcibly determined. Everyone should therefore have the freedom to break out of this straitjacket, and "no eligibility criteria . . . [should] be a prerequisite for changing one's name, legal sex, or gender,"[21] as this would amount to an attack on the inalienable right to authenticity now promised to everyone. This philosophy has also inspired the emerging field of "fat studies," which argues that "fatphobia," like other forms of discrimination, systematically stigmatizes obese people, particularly through the medical perspective that considers obesity to be a disease or a health hazard.[22] The advantage enjoyed by the authentic self therefore allows it to deconstruct imperatives as objective as those of biology and health.

Nevertheless, it is in relation to non-Western cultures and religions that the ethics of authenticity has spread most widely in the last half-century. Particularly in the Anglosphere, it has led to virulent hostility toward criticism of radical Islam and the French laws to contain it, which are described as a despicable repression of authenticity by a chauvinistic form of intolerance. Martha Nussbaum describes banning the burqa in public as an unfair law that "tacitly favors majority practices and burdens minority practices."[23] Banning religious symbols such as the Islamic veil in public services would therefore be outright discrimination that would force believers to live in an inauthentic way. Similarly, there would be absolutely nothing scandalous about young girls being forced by their parents or community to wear the burqa: this falls "in the same category as all sorts of requirements, pleasant and unpleasant, that parents impose on their children: wearing 'respectable' clothing, going to the 'right' school, getting top grades, practicing the violin, dating only people of the 'right' religion, getting into a top college."[24] Relations with minority religions should therefore be guided above all by non-coercion and accommodation of "authenticity," even for practices that are carried out by a small, radicalized minority:

> For religions such as Islam that contain many different views about what is required, and its spirit is attractive: if an individual sincerely believes that wearing a burqa is required . . ., it does no good to point out that many co-religionists disagree.[25]

Radical Islam imposed on children would therefore not be tyranny, but a mark of authenticity. If the ethic of authenticity can afford to be so permissive toward practices that are inegalitarian or even opposed to the fundamentals of science as we understand it today, it is because it does not constitute a reflection on what is right on a collective scale, concerned with achieving a balance that allows everyone to live together in a pluralistic society. On the contrary, it is primarily embodied as a principle of deconstruction, which systematically gives primacy to eccentricity over the norm, because the further a practice or claim deviates from the mainstream, the more it is considered "authentic" in its eyes. Once this slippery slope begins, this claim is unsurprisingly extended to all socially condemned "lifestyle choices," such as drug addiction, prostitution, or refusal to work:[26]

> Don't our character, our personality, and our worldviews also belong to the set of things that do not depend on us and that we are not free to change as we please? Is it not just as repugnant

> to judge someone on the basis of character as it is to judge them on the basis of race?[27]

Through the prism of authenticity, an established cultural tradition is always likely to conflict with the self. Contemporary liberalism therefore adopts a minimalist morality, based on Mill's principle that the freedom of one person ends where that of another begins. However, its application is more complex than it seems, because in the "society of identities," where self-restraint no longer exists, conflicts will inevitably arise between people's authentic personalities. The state therefore retains the difficult task of arbitrating conflicts, but now does so hypocritically, through "subversive" conformism.

Subversive Conformity

The promise of the ethics of authenticity, through the unmediated expression of everyone's self, is in trouble when multiple forms of authenticity clash. Thus, the deconstruction of laws that promote a majority lifestyle is not enough to its advocates, because established norms still exist in the common practices of ordinary people, which are just as detrimental to minority authenticity and therefore should be regulated:

> In short, liberals are against any state moral policing. But they have nothing against private moral policing. However, in my opinion, there is no reason not to apply the political principle of suspending public authorities' judgment of what people do with their own lives, as long as they do not directly and intentionally harm others, to the moral judgments of each and every individual. Should those who condemn state racism or homophobia be more lenient towards ordinary racism or homophobia?[28]

If character and personality traits are as much a part of authenticity as gender or ethnicity, why should private opinions, however questionable, be suppressed in the name of freedom? How am I respecting the authenticity of others if I force them to call me by a certain pronoun against their better judgment? Demanding that companies or governments practice so-called "affirmative action" is also disrespectful of employers' autonomy to hire whomever they wish. The proliferation of safe spaces, where certain words can no longer be spoken, or "single-sex meetings," from which certain groups are formally excluded, demonstrates that the primacy of authenticity leads to a clash of subjectivities. Contrary to what it claims, Mill's harm principle can never be exercised without harming someone; it always ends up discriminating.[29] In the countercultural context, it is about the freedom of the marginalized individual, who is not to be protected from other individuals as equals, but from "unprotected" people and the prejudices they convey, in a one-way logic. This is why the City of Montreal was considering mandating "anti-rumor agents to break down prejudices against immigrants," whose job would be to intervene "with people who convey stereotypes,"[30] an "inclusive public moral police" to combat the ignorance attributed to the common man.

In the age of authenticity, the law no longer plays the role of collective reason bringing individual passions to order; rather, it defends the self against a disciplinary society accused of undermining its autonomy. It is society that is not made for man and that should be changed from above. Conversely, a state that returned to the sources of the democratic ideal and imposed necessary concessions on individual authenticity to ensure the unity of the social body would represent "a form of oppression, imprisoning someone in a false, distorted, and reduced mode of being."[31] Since judgment is prescriptive and enforces social norms, it must be suspended in an amoral society, where only freedom of choice is valid. The absence of judgment becomes a civic requirement and, above all, a dogma that the state vehemently protects.[32] Freed from the duty to embody the values of a particular nation, the utmost goal of public authority would now be moral "neutrality." It is required to "live and let live" on a large scale . . . and to bring those who refuse into line.

This implies the abandonment of any cultural role for the state. Caricatured as "state-sponsored cultural traditionalism,"[33] the idea that a nation can have its own culture, promoted by the public authorities no less, arouses fear, particularly in the Anglosphere. An official language or classic works to be learned by all in middle school would be seen as authoritarian and a breach of the public duty of indifference. According to American political scientist Paul D. Miller, a state that defends a particular nation would be equivalent to "Jim Crow on a global scale, an insistence that cultural majorities have a presumptive right to defend their culture with the power of the state, a right that cultural minorities lack for no other reason than being in a minority."[34] Moreover, the very history of Western countries becomes an obstacle to the promotion of their own values of diversity and inclusion: the majority culture and its past are deemed insufficiently "diverse." This is why a truly anachronistic pluralism is emerging in school textbooks, museums, and historical representations. One need only think of recent TV shows that depict medieval Europe with the ethnic composition of contemporary Brooklyn.

The end of the nation-state is also being accelerated by two converging movements: the sanctification of the "right to migrate" and the prohibition on requiring immigrants to integrate, let alone assimilate. French libertarian philosopher Ruwen Ogien claims that there is indeed a sacralized individual right not to live in the country where we were born, which necessarily imposes "a correlative duty to welcome those who emigrate."[35] This duty would take precedence over the right of Western nations to preserve their own authentic identity, which is rarely, if ever, defended in the progressive camp. Multiculturalist thinkers explain that cultural norms are a metaphorical "cage"[36] in which it would be cruel to lock up migrants and that, on the contrary, "enabling integration may require some modification of the institutions of the dominant culture."[37] While it was generally assumed that integration was legitimate and that it implied adapting to the majority lifestyle in the public sphere without extinguishing particularism in the private sphere, its critics claim that it is "reproducing a colonial worldview."[38] Integration is said to be inherently conservative, as it implies a "reduction of diversity" that runs counter to the ethic of authenticity: "as a result of crossing that border, the immigrant needs to change, to be or do something in relation to whatever it is they must integrate into to achieve the desired parity."[39] On the other hand, non-Western peoples, such as the Kanaks of New Caledonia, would be entirely justified in defending their identity, with the approval of leading left-wing figures such as French former socialist minister Christiane Taubira: "A people on this land refuses to decline, to wither away, to die out. That's how nations are: attached to their roots, their cultures, their myths."[40]

The promotion of authenticity has become an inconsistent logic that too often boils down to giving priority to "protected groups," who have the privilege of differentiated rights, over ordinary people who do not. Is it still possible to freely choose tradition and yet remain authentic? Because it draws a distinction between the rebel and the conformist, rather than between choice and lack of choice, counterculture answers in the negative: "He who lets the world, or his own portion of it, choose his plan of life for him, has no need of any other faculty than the ape-like one of imitation. He who chooses his plan for himself, employs all his faculties."[41] According to Mill, if one is truly human, one cannot be ordinary, conformist, and even less conservative. He thus comes close to the nihilistic idea that it is only by doing evil, or at least what is not expected of him by the prevailing norms, that man can prove that he is free, whether in relation to God or to society: "It is man's moral freedom that produces evil. Nowhere is this more evident than when it becomes the will to do evil. Sin becomes the ultimate symbol of the creature's power over itself in relation to its creator."[42] This is a paradox of individuality: to prove that I am free, I must obey my impulses, which take away my ability to choose.

As anti-conformism hardens into a new conformity, we are now hearing more voices condemn the progressive "new puritans" for betraying the ideal of freedom in order to establish a moral framework that is as restrictive as the old one. The condemnation is not a challenge to counterculture from the outside. It is an argument within it. And because counterculture still relies on the same scapegoats—conservatism and "the old moral order"—it is far less transgressive than it thinks:

> Not long ago, imposing a moral framework on every aspect of life was a conservative predilection. It was the right wing didn't like the music you listened to, the television you watched, or the tabloid trash you read. It was the right that identified antisocial themes in seemingly harmless entertainment products that only they, with their keen senses of propriety, could discern. It was the right that saw the world through a moral prism, and it was the right that policed violations of its preferred ethical framework with vigor.[43]

To formulate this objection, one must assume the possibility of a middle ground, completely neutral in terms of values, which would oppose two moral orders, conservatism and progressivism. It would be the regime of freedom, while the others would be regimes of constraint. However, a society without an ethical framework does not exist, and never has. Behind any claim to freedom, whatever it may be, lies the desire to apply it and to deviate from the current norm. While this desire is sometimes justified, it is never selfless. Authenticity in itself becomes especially hypocritical because it condemns its subjects to a pernicious hypocrisy that dares not say its name.

Domus* and *Forum

By elevating authenticity, our era has become particularly harsh on hypocrisy, which has become synonymous with dishonesty and malice. In the same way, the demand that certain subjectivities regulate themselves appears inauthentic, even violent. Yet, French economist Olivier Babeau reminds us that hypocrisy is "the secret foundation of human society," "both the condition for and the manifestation of civilization itself."[44] What he calls the public virtue of hypocrisy corresponds, in fact, to a kind of "softening filter," that of the customs through which subjectivity must pass in order to express itself in a way that is compatible with the common good. This virtuous duplicity "consisted of putting up with unwelcome presences, smiling at and welcoming annoying people, knowing how to listen to talkative old bores, and concealing one's impatience. This was called being polite."[45]

Basic courtesy, a precious achievement of the civilizing process, constitutes a voluntary limitation on the expression of our inner selves in the interest of the whole, which goes hand in hand with virtues such as modesty and discretion. These seem to be disappearing today. In this era of uncompromising freedom, this restraint, "which forbids us in society from indulging in activities that, however pleasant they may be for us, could legitimately be a nuisance to others,"[46] no longer has any reason to exist in the eyes of many. Why refrain from listening to loud music on public transport? Why bother dressing neatly for work when you only dress for yourself? Why listen to and respect the opinions of others if you already know you are right? What is now commonly referred to as "incivility," like the increasingly intense polarization of political debates, is part of this uncompromising trend. It ignores a basic truth pointed out by sociologist Richard Sennett: identity, like behavior, is a "meeting point between who a person wants to be and what the world allows him to be."[47] By removing the second part of the equation, the ethics of authenticity deconstructs a founding principle of liberal democracy: the separation of public and private life. Modern citizenship effectively implies a basic restriction on the authenticity of each individual, who cannot act in the same way in private as in public:

> The separation of public and private thus became a founding principle of the social order: the private sphere was reserved for the freedom of individuals in all their diversity, while the public sphere was reserved for the affirmation of equal rights for citizens. All particularities were relegated to the private sphere. Citizenship is based on the opposition between the specificities of the private individual, a member of civil society, and the universality of the citizen.[48]

Even among liberals such as John Rawls, this idea of the fundamental duality of the citizen remains. In *Political Liberalism*, when he considers the conditions for a peaceful society, Rawls stipulates that each citizen must, in addition to the "comprehensive doctrine" that constitutes their own way of envisaging what constitutes a successful life, possess a conception of politics that concerns the common good. In other words, one cannot meld the public sphere and the private sphere and act in the same way in both contexts: "The political is distinct from the associational, which is voluntary in ways that the political is not; it is also distinct from the personal and the familial, which are affectional, again in ways the political is not."[49] Without this universality specific to the public sphere, society would collapse under the conflicts and contradictions of immoderate impulses and identities.

In modern times, the nation has asserted itself as the main "noble lie," in Plato's words, which has enabled societies to hold together. Critics of the national form who point to its "artificial homogeneity"[50] or who are scandalized that the dark parts of national history are not showcased have completely misunderstood its historical and political function. Contrary to what we might think today, national belonging is not self-evident; it is a political and cultural construct that has been built up over a long period of time, and above all, it is the best way that human beings have found to overcome blood loyalties in order to find a peaceful way of living together.[51] Sharing a language, history, and customs makes it possible to accept pluralism, particularly ideological pluralism, in the name of what unites citizens, and thus to avoid civil war. This is what provides the "preexisting We" that is essential to democracy, without which it would be impossible to conjugate "the people" in the singular and claim that they express their unified will at the ballot box. In Benedict Anderson's famous words, it is an "imagined community,"[52] but it is nonetheless real and most valuable.

Contemporary defenders of authenticity are skeptical of the national form and the imperatives it entails. In a so-called open society, transparency breaks down the salutary wall between the private and the public, on the grounds that "the personal is political," according to the famous sixties slogan. The intention to bring certain injustices that can occur in private life—such as domestic violence—into the public debate is necessary, but it should in no way lead to the end of the separation between the two spheres. Critics of privacy forget that it represents the ultimate sphere of freedom, the only place where we can all be fully ourselves without having to answer to anyone. The fact that our homes are sanctuaries where we can express our innermost thoughts and, more generally, behave as we see fit, is a blessing that very few would want to do without. This is the meaning of the distinction between *domus*, the home, and *forum*, the public space, which is the foundation of the free world. If the public infiltrates the private, then the sanctity of the home is broken: personal choices cease to be personal, because they take on a political dimension on which everyone can have a say, since they now belong to the public sphere.

Particularly in hyper-politicized times such as ours, the "shrinking of privacy" is a danger to social cohesion.[53] Since 2010, with the rise of the Occupy movement, and even more since 2015, with #MeToo and Black Lives Matter, we have been living in an extremely politicized era, where identity politics are omnipresent in the media.[54] While the French protesters of May '68 chanted "*vie privée, privé de vie*" (private life, deprived of life), today the slogan "*silence is violence*" expresses this activist enrollment from which it is impossible to escape, lest one fall on the wrong side of neo-conformism. This was particularly the case with the #BlackOutTuesday movement, which urged everyone to share a black square in memory of George Floyd on their social media accounts, resulting in an authoritarian pressure on those who had not followed the injunction, whether intentionally or not.[55] The omnipresence of identity activism has conquered sports, TV series,[56] and even advertising, with Gillette razors lecturing Americans on "toxic masculinity" and gender ideology.[57] This ubiquity causes average citizens to feel that politics is everywhere, and that there is no escape from never-ending culture wars. The recession of a depoliticized private sphere coincides with the rise of a public sphere stripped of discussion about the common good, as it is overloaded with everyone's narrow identities.

Equality through the Common Good

Authenticity as a social principle is a risky bet, taking identities out of the private sphere to turn them into public banners. Perversely, the complete politicization of life inevitably leads to the loss of personality: individuals cease to be singular as they are transformed into "representatives" of their respective groups. By claiming to free us from the burden of public hypocrisy, authenticity "requires each of us to be what we appear to be,"[58] which is all the more insidious. The idea of "diverse representation," often used as a euphemism to refer to non-white people, embodies this pernicious flaw in identity politics. The individual is no longer important once he or she becomes a "representative" of his or her color, sexual orientation, faith, or any other group that erases his or her own personality. Contrary to what fashionable progressivism would have us believe, they lose their freedom, because they are no longer free to be themselves; they become activists enlisted in the service of a cause, who must do what is expected of them in order to be a "good representative." Québécois conservative politician Éric Duhaime, in a book on his homosexuality, shares these reservations. He explains that he has never spoken publicly about his sexual preferences before, precisely because he refuses to make it a "public" issue and considers it a matter of his personal life:

> This is the first time I have publicly mentioned my sexual orientation. I have resisted all temptations, all invitations . . . I refused to talk about it in the media because I am not a gay activist. My sexual orientation is just one of the things that characterizes me, not an ideology I adhere to . . . Above all, I don't want to be defined first and foremost by the gender of the person I sleep with . . . I also feel that displaying our differences automatically makes us spokespersons or standard-bearers for the cause. I certainly don't want to be one![59]

He is right to fear a completely politicized world, where everyone's identities would be constantly debated in the public arena. Once an identity leaves the private sphere to become a political cause or banner, the entire political community has a say in what was previously a matter of personal choice. If "the private sphere is my business, and therefore no one else's,"[60] it ceases to be private when demonstrations are organized in its name, when it is shouted from the rooftops, and when those who are not concerned are forced to take a position.

The strategy of highlighting differences has not always had positive results. On the contrary, Robert Putnam, the great American theorist of social capital, points to a fact often overlooked by contemporary identity activists: while cohesion and the sense of unity it generates lead to equality, emphasizing differences creates a "clash of authenticities," which often leads to a backlash in attitudes between groups. In *The Upswing*, Putnam highlights the "hidden progress" of the first half of the twentieth century in the United States for women's and African American rights, which has disappeared from collective memory since it was overshadowed by the activism of the sixties. While the pre-1960 era is now considered a "dark age" for the rights of everyone except white men, followed by spontaneous progress that finally brought equality, the story is quite different.

In fact, the fifty years preceding contemporary activism, driven by a strong ethic of conformity and duty, coincided with major changes in general attitudes toward Black people and women, a product of greater social and national cohesion. In terms of health, education, economic prospects, and voter turnout, African Americans experienced a marked and rapid improvement in their conditions, but above all, racist attitudes toward them among white Americans declined dramatically. While in 1940 only 30 percent of white Americans supported integrated schools, this proportion jumped to almost 70 percent in the early 1960s.[61] Similarly, support for equality between men and women in the workplace and in politics increased dramatically until 1970, when it reached a plateau.[62] In both cases, solidarity born of the war effort, where men mixed ethnically in the army and women entered factories *en masse*, is often cited as a turning point in social attitudes. It was therefore solidarity and rallying around a common cause that paved the way for equality, not pitting groups against one another.

Thus, the civil rights gained in the last half-century are less of a revolution in attitudes (which had changed before) than the law catching up with social mores. Without the social capital and egalitarian vision produced by the cohesion of the early twentieth century, these social movements would never have been possible—public opinion would not have allowed it. The idea that all citizens are part of the same nation, in pursuit of the common good, is, on the contrary, a powerful driver of equality. In other words, society had to already be moving toward equality for inequality to be shocking:

> In many ways, it was very the progress women *had* made before the 1960s that fueled growing discontent with these inegalitarian realities. Ever-greater numbers of women were reaching adulthood educated, ambitious, and independent-minded, only to find their agency and options artificially curtailed.[63]

The progress made since the 1960s and 1970s, such as the evolution of laws giving full legal status to women and Black Americans, or the greater representation of minorities in many leadership positions, was the product of societies already engaged in a dynamic of equality. It was precisely in light of this progress that legal discrimination appeared anachronistic and was eventually abolished. If we want to judge the fruits of the ethics of authenticity, we should instead look at the resurgence of differentialism over the past ten years:

since 2014–2015, there has been a marked reversal in satisfaction with racial relations in the United States. If 55 percent of citizens were satisfied in 2014, 70 percent were dissatisfied in 2021.[64] It is not the objective conditions of minorities that have deteriorated during this time, but the tone of the conversation on equality and discrimination, poisoned by a resentful discourse. The same could be said of relations between men and women: the rise of reactionary masculinism via Andrew Tate, a notorious influencer among young men and a convicted sex trafficker, comes at the same time as a vocal fringe of feminism that unashamedly asserts that "men are trash."[65] In the eyes of conservative feminist Mary Harrington, these are two sides of the same "gender separatism," which does not bode well.[66]

The current deterioration of public debate is the direct result of a "clash of authenticities." Those authenticities no longer pass through the mediation of civilizing social norms. Unsurprisingly, the deconstruction of rules that tempered everyone's subjectivity, and the tarnishing of the nation as a rallying point for all citizens, has not created greater solidarity among citizens of Western countries. In order to relearn how to live together, we must leave behind the strategy of confrontation and return to that of cohesion, which creates sympathy and unity beyond differences. The political left has failed this important test by gradually dissociating itself from the figure of the people and instead focusing on criticizing the common good through the politics of recognition.

CHAPTER 4

What Is Left of the Left?

THE COUNTERCULTURAL SHIFT that took place in the 1960s had profound consequences on left-wing thinking. Once it had integrated into a comfortable social order and abandoned its revolutionary whims, the proletariat could no longer serve as the historical subject of a revolutionary project set against the norms that structure society. The "woke revolution" of the 2010s marked the culmination of this doctrinal transformation, by symbolically excluding the Western middle classes from the progressive camp in favor of a coalition of identity groups whose only commonality was that they did not conform to the norm—that they were "the Other." American universities became the epicenter of a new progressive discourse, continuing the long-standing critique of Western history and values. The new discourse quickly spread outside of campus, through events such as the politicization of George Floyd's death. Rather than taking the side of the individual against constraint or conformism, wokeism speaks out on behalf of so-called marginalized communities, the new revolutionary subject, to renew the left after the fall of Marxism.

Marcuse: The Left without Its Revolutionary Subject

The fall from grace of the people, from revolutionary subject to potential tyrant, led to the collapse of the Marxist vision of the world, which seems almost conservative today compared to what the left has become. The communist project, at least in appearance, was part of the culture of conformity and revolved around a celebration of workers and the normality they embodied. In *The Communist Manifesto*, Marx and Engels seem aware of the popular aspiration for stability when they denounce that "the bourgeoisie cannot exist without constantly revolutionizing the instruments of production, and thereby the relations of production, and with them the whole relations of society."[1] Faced with the prospect of incessant upheavals in existence by a predatory class, the end of history was "to raise the proletariat to the position of ruling class, to win the battle of democracy,"[2] and thus to establish a stable society where workers receive fair compensation for their labor. Marx and Engels also harbored a certain nostalgia for "certain types of community—the family, the neighborhood, and the guild—found in the world of peasants and artisans, which, with the violent advent of competitive society, were in the process of collapsing, and whose disappearance was experienced as a loss."[3]

Part of the appeal that communism long held for the working classes was the idea of placing ordinary people at the center of a stable order designed for the hard-working majority rather than the wealthy minority. In this respect, it was to some extent in line with the democratic aspirations of modernity. From today's perspective, one can almost be amazed at "how modest the Marxian critique of society was compared to the countercultural critique."[4] It was so modest that the social democracy that emerged from the postwar economic boom was largely able to accommodate the critique, to the point of creating a real existential crisis on the left.

The German-American Marxist philosopher Herbert Marcuse was one of the major thinkers of the counterculture in the sixties. When he published *One-Dimensional Man* in 1964, the revolutionary project was stalling. The rise of the welfare state had calmed, if not extinguished, demands for radical change in the social order through social policies that greatly enriched the middle class. Faced with an affluent society that "seems increasingly capable of satisfying the needs of the individuals through the way in which it is organized," "critical theory is left without the rationale for transcending this society."[5] Rather than rejoicing in the obsolescence of Marxism, Marcuse seeks to rescue critical thinking and find new ways to undermine the established order. He demonstrated a greater attachment to the ideal of overturning the social order than to its ends, which were to enable workers to benefit more or less equitably from collective wealth, even through reformist means.

Marcuse therefore breaks with Marxism by diagnosing the "weakening of the negative position of the working class: it no longer appears to be the living contradiction of the established society,"[6] because it benefits from social democracy and has no interest in seeing this system overthrown. He therefore sought a new class, a substitute proletariat that would embody the negation of the political order, and found it in marginalized groups:

> . . . underneath the conservative popular base is the substratum of the outcasts and outsiders, the exploited and persecuted of other races and other colors, the unemployed and the unemployable. They exist outside the democratic process; their life is the most immediate and the most real need for ending intolerable conditions and institutions. Thus their opposition is revolutionary even if their consciousness is not.[7]

The significance of this change in Western political life cannot be underestimated. French philosopher Laurent Bouvet calls the reversal of the figure of the majority in the left-wing imagination, shifting from "the collective emancipation of the majority of the population . . . against domination by a minority" to "individual emancipation based on rights related to identity criteria deemed 'dominated' or 'discriminated against' . . . defining minorities . . . against the majority of the population."[8]

When the left had to choose between its concern for the majority and its drive to overturn the social order, it leaned toward the latter and thus shifted from democracy to elitism. Marcuse's project is an elitist revolution that recognizes itself as such, the dictatorship of an enlightened caste that manipulates the liberal framework to exclude its ideological opponents. Marcuse contrasts supposedly repressive tolerance, which allows everyone the right to speak, with "liberating tolerance," or "intolerance against movements from the Right and toleration of movements from the Left," which he then characterizes as "the 'official' promotion of subversion."[9] As Mathieu Bock-Côté explains, he revealed that his struggle was not for the material prosperity of ordinary people, but rather for the overthrow of the social order: "Progressivism is a revelation that the civilization in which we live is radically unacceptable."

What needed to be kept alive was "critical theory," the ideal of emancipation from the social order, not the idea of improving the lives of workers. Marcuse abandoned the people to save the revolution, prioritizing "a critical view of the existing order before any specific vision of the future."[10] In this manner, the woke left, rather than breaking with the traditional left, constitutes a purification and radicalization of the revolution. Faced with the possible end of history, it tried to preserve the essence of what communist intellectuals held dear, namely, all-out opposition to the established order. This is why the most accurate definition of wokeism, given by

French intellectual Pierre Valentin, is based primarily on a critique of the West:

> Wokeism is an ideology that perceives Western societies as being fundamentally governed by power structures, hierarchies of domination, and systems of oppression whose goal, or at least effect, is to subordinate the Other—that is, minorities in all their forms (sexual, religious, ethnic, etc.), often by invisible means.[11]

The only guiding principle that adequately sums up this ideology remains its negative function: wokeism is defined first and foremost by what it fights against, not what it stands for, which can change at will. Its revolutionary subject remains that of Marcuse, namely "the substratum of outcasts and outsiders,"[12] which only achieves this status because it embodies the contradiction of the social order, because it finds itself on its margins. The idea of a "negative unity" or "common-enemy identity politics"[13] emphasizes this fact: the political left, which has replaced the proletariat, now seeks to unite those who contradict the figure of the Western majority, on this sole basis. While this change is significant in relation to socialism, it does not seem substantial enough to mark a difference in nature, to erect "the fiction of an insurmountable wall between leftism and wokeism."[14] A direct link connects the two ideologies, one being the logical continuation of the other, after the proletariat has been surpassed. With a new subject and a new metanarrative, wokeism applies the internal logic of the old left but broadens the spectrum to include identity issues, rather than confining itself to economics alone.

In 1984, Chantal Mouffe and Ernesto Laclau published *Hegemony and Socialist Strategy*, a pioneering essay which theorized for the first time the so-called intersectional approach on the left, or the addition of all marginal identity struggles into a single "chain of equivalences," a common front of those "excluded" from the social order.[15] This strategy is based on the assumption that progressive demands, whether anti-racist, LGBT, feminist, or even animal rights, complement each other insofar as they have a common adversary, the figure of the universal subject of modern democracy, caricatured as the dominant white male:

> This "convergence of oppressions" points to the emblematic figure of the dominant, in which "man" and "human" (but also "adult" or "white") tend to merge into a single multifaceted identity. Many commentators have thus noted that the figure of the sovereign subject of Modernity, the figure of the rational and self-controlled human being, which corresponds to that of the adult white (male) man, is defined in a very similar way in opposition to animality, femininity, and childhood.[16]

We can therefore see that left-wing discourse, by explaining so clearly what it is fighting against, systematizes the countercultural matrix within a rigid framework. In its own way, it defends the figure of the individual alone against disciplinary society, in the form of the "abnormal subject" rejected by norms. On one side, we find an oppressive and omnipotent system, and on the other, its victims.

A Systemic Way of Thinking

The struggle between the dominant and the dominated, according to the left-wing interpretation of the world, takes place within an all-powerful system, where the dice are loaded in favor of the dominant. This system can be white supremacy, patriarchy, heteronormativity, cisnormativity—all the normative systems that ensure the primacy of the Normal over the Abnormal. Philosophers Luc Ferry and Alain

Renaut described this tendency to see the system as "the real subject of history,"[17] thus erasing individual experiences and realities. Above all, insofar as the system to be deconstructed remains the constant in the multiple variations of the same discourse, it is the system itself that is at the center, much more so than the groups it uses to problematize it.

The theory of deconstruction, in order to target its adversary, begins by "unveiling and defining an ideology, then explaining that it is the foundation of our perception of things and that it conditions our way of seeing the world."[18] The individual, who has no contact outside the encompassing system, no longer exists, nor does the universal, because everything becomes a social construct, a creation of the system that filters access to reality. "Systemic" domination validates itself through any statistical disparity, which is assumed to be the result of malicious intent rather than individual choices or logically explicable realities. Political scientist Yascha Mounk calls this "disparitarianism,"[19] a view that interprets any statistical difference as the result of discrimination that must be corrected from the top-down. However, disparitarianism remains selective in its reading of statistics: if certain cultural minorities are "overrepresented" in prison, this is seen as a sign of systemic racism, but no one would have the absurd idea of claiming that the vast majority of prisoners are men because of systemic misandry.

In the eyes of systemic thinking, objective truth no longer exists: the system is so totalitarian that what appears to be the truth is in fact digested and reworked by ideology and serves to reinforce the power of the dominant over the dominated. Reality is therefore systematically approached with suspicion, a Marxist legacy that Roger Scruton calls "the habit of going behind."[20] What is said is no longer important; only who says it matters, because that is how we can guess whose interests they serve. We cannot trust individuals to be altruistic, as they are prisoners of their own interests, which they will always defend. This is the "theory of positioning," according to which members of oppressed groups all share the same experience, which is unique to them and remains incomprehensible to their oppressors because of their opposite positioning, which predestines them to want to perpetuate the oppressive system of which they are the beneficiaries.[21] As Foucault says: "interpretation will always henceforth be an interpretation by the 'Who?'; we do not interpret what is in the signified, but we interpret at the bottom: who made the interpretation."[22] Communication changes meaning: rather than serving to link different realities and promote understanding, it becomes "a sublimation of power relations or, if you will, a euphemized form of war."[23]

This theory seems appealing because it has an answer for everything. It "can only consider the objections raised against it as resistance, in the analytical sense of the term, and therefore as further confirmation of its truth."[24] If systemic racism, for example, is questioned by a white person, it is a manifestation of "white fragility,"[25] proof that the dominant group is defending its interests and refusing to listen to the reality of the dominated. Conversely, if a Black person questions the theory, they thereby demonstrate their "false consciousness,"[26] a concept already used by Marx to discard proletarians who did not subscribe to his theory. This analytical framework has the attributes of a conspiracy theory: any fact that could call it into question is swallowed up in a totalizing system. More strangely, however, it is a conspiracy without conspirators: ideology so deeply permeates social norms that it is reproduced without anyone realizing it. It would be possible to live in a systemically racist society without any individual member being racist, as long as the aggregate effect of social interactions produces unsatisfactory results from a disparitarian perspective.[27]

Is it surprising that the COVID-19 pandemic has attracted so many left-leaning people to the conspiracy theories? The socialist imagination is naturally inclined toward conspiracies, primarily in its conception of "capitalism," which is not the sum of private interactions, but rather a moving beast with a consciousness of its own, constantly giving birth to new variations: surveillance capitalism, disaster capitalism, racial capitalism, emotional capitalism, and prison capitalism, among others.[28] It should therefore come as no surprise that a left-wing thinker as widely read and renowned as the Italian philosopher Giorgio Agamben began spreading the idea, from the very first days of the pandemic, that it was in fact a pure invention designed to increase control over citizens: "With terrorism exhausted as a cause for exceptional measures, the invention of an epidemic [offers] the ideal pretext for extending (exceptional measures) beyond all limits."[29] Hiding behind the rhetoric of conspiracy without conspirators, Agamben sums up in his fantasized description of COVID the systemic thinking within the left-wing matrix: "There are conspiracies that are, so to speak, objective, which seem to function as such without being directed by an identifiable subject."

Naomi Klein, uncomfortable with the words of Agamben, nevertheless realizes that he is orthodoxly applying her own analytical framework. While she maintains that "there are always systemic forces at play," the mistake of conspiracy theorists, especially those on the right, has been to believe that it is a cabal of evil individuals perverting an otherwise just democracy, rather than "a system doing what it was designed to do, no matter the human cost." In other words, the right is not sufficiently conspiracy-minded for Klein, as it fails to see the larger system behind individual wills, which it still holds responsible for the course of the world: "without a firm understanding of capitalism's drive to find profit sources to enclose and extract, many imagine there is a cabal of uniquely nefarious individuals pulling the strings."[30] Conspiracy without conspirators is the preferred form of systemic thinking. Rather than pointing the finger at individuals, it blames the whole of civilization, accusing it of operating in a diffuse and therefore all the more insidious manner.

The Weaponization of the Concern for Victims

If left-wing discourse is still alive after the end of the proletariat and continues to persist in the Western consciousness to this day, it is because it draws on powerful emotions, foremost among which is what René Girard calls "concern for victims," deeply ingrained in the Judeo-Christian consciousness. Marxism and its ideological descendants cannot therefore be reduced to a force external to the West, an exogenous virus that spontaneously infected it. On the contrary, as Raymond Aron explains, this ideology "is an integral part of European thought"[31] and plays on the deepest springs of Western emotions. In a way, "Marxism has done nothing but promise us paradise on earth, that is, to build this exit from history here below instead of waiting for it beyond,"[32] because the Christian God is the God of the poor, who identifies himself with those in positions of weakness: "Inasmuch as ye have done it unto one of the least of these my brethren, ye have done it unto me." While the idea of concern for victims is deeply rooted in civilization, its contemporary application is entirely new:

> Our society is the most preoccupied with victims of any that ever was. Even if it is insincere, a big show, the phenomenon has no precedent. No historical period, no society we know, has ever spoken of victims as we do. We can detect in the recent past the beginnings of the contemporary attitude, but every day new records are broken. We are all actors as well as witnesses in a great anthropological first. Examine ancient sources, inquire everywhere, dig up the corners of the planet, and you will

> not find anything anywhere that even remotely resembles our modern concern for victims.[33]

The movement that reversed the meanings of freedom and democracy has done the same with concern for victims, which now goes against its original intention. Loving one's neighbor was based primarily on proximity, as was defending "the least of [one's] brethren." The Christian figure of the victim is the most disadvantaged part of the collective, toward whom we have a duty of solidarity by virtue of our common humanity. It was because they were part of the nation and contributed to its growth that workers were able to demand the welfare state, not because they were on its margins. The fathers of the American Revolution's plea for democracy did not rely on the marginality of Americans. On the contrary, they argued that there could be "no taxation without representation" because citizens were doing the work and paying the taxes without which society could not function, and thus deserved to be recognized proportionally to their contribution to the common good.

Anti-civilization shapes a reverse concern for victims: the defense of the Other as Other. This matrix disrupts the relationship with the weakest, who gain status linked to their otherness rather than to their similarity to their fellow citizens. Bradley Campbell and Jason Manning thus speak of a "victimhood culture," where suffering confers privileged social status. Paradoxically, real power, social consideration, and legitimacy now come from the absence of power.[34] Logically, there is a desire to gain the status of the oppressed fighting against an overpowering structure, and more and more people are seeking to frame their own actions in the countercultural narrative, as defined in the previous chapter: the eccentric self fighting the disciplinary society. What Jonathan Haidt calls the emotional register of care and suffering[35] is what confers the greatest legitimacy in society. For a claim to be heard and taken seriously today, it should be translated into the language of suffering. Consider the rhetoric that now prevails on university campuses that certain unpopular ideas could cause "suffering," to the extent that simply stating them would cause such significant damage that the speaker should be censored. We can bet that if the censors spoke in the language of authority and said instead, "the university is our intellectual territory and you will not set foot in it," they would not enjoy the same sympathy as they now do. It is by portraying themselves as being at the bottom of the power chain that they can reach the top and dictate which ideas are acceptable and which are not.

The true indicator of the privileged status of victims today is undoubtedly the competition for victimhood, where actors seek to show themselves to be "more victimized than others" in order to symbolically win the debate and be absolved of any fault. If the language of suffering is the one that gives access to power and recognition, we should not be surprised that some people now claim to be marginalized in order to reap the privileges that come with this status. Rather than wanting to join the center of society, people want to flee it, because that is where moral superiority lies. Just think of the celebrities who claim to be Native American without a drop of native blood, such as singer Buffy Sainte-Marie, icon of the 1960s hippie movement, who was in fact Italian-American. The many stories of people inventing false "hate crimes" against themselves to gain public sympathy underscore this same disturbing fact.[36] Why would anyone want to become a victim if there were no social benefits to be gained?

The tragedy in all of this is that the idealization of victims has come at the expense of the admirable figure of the hero, which has lost its prominence. Unlike the contemporary victim, who is born a victim because of their marginalized identity, the hero is a person like any other, who has made themselves who they are through their heroic deeds and who, even more so, protects their less fortunate brothers.[37] They carry within them the promise of an exceptional destiny for anyone who wishes to do good and accomplish great things. One is not born a hero; one becomes one. This figure, which contradicts the logic of eternal polarization between the dominant and the dominated, is now viewed with suspicion on the left. Behind every great hero, there is said to be a great crime. Attempts to banish Winston Churchill, Christopher Columbus, and other great men of Western civilization are part of the extension of this logic: If victim status becomes the sole source of legitimacy, then heroes can no longer be celebrated, since the reasons for their greatness conflict with the great narrative of the times.

As Girard says, "The victims most interesting to us are always those who allow us to condemn our neighbors. And our neighbors do the same. They always think first about victims for whom they hold us responsible."[38] In a culture of victimhood, the most effective way to attack someone is to rhetorically tip them into the camp of the oppressors. If they have victims to their name, they can then be criticized. This principle is at the heart of left-wing rhetoric, which constantly broadens the margins it exploits in order to better invalidate the center of society, described as the source of all oppressions.

The Expanding Circle of the Marginalized

As demonstrated by the movement initiated by Marcuse from the proletariat to the marginalized, the logic of the left is fluid; it cannot be static in order to fulfill its vocation of perpetual criticism of the established order. Because it is above all negative, it is its "historical mission" to extend "the circle of human sympathy"[39] ever further from the figure of the norm. Peter Singer defends this thesis in *The Expanding Circle*: there is something intrinsically expansionist in the nature of reason, which legitimizes the increasing decentralization of the moral community in the name of new classes of oppressed people. The task would therefore be to push back the margins and find "those who see the social order from the outside, from the position of domination they suffer," in a "constantly renewed critique of Western civilization, to push it ever further into self-criticism and convert it to its own deconstruction."[40] If their condition were to improve to the point where they were no longer sufficiently subversive, the excluded of yesterday would suffer the same fate as the proletariat and be discarded as supporters of the system.

It is from this logic of transcending boundaries that Singer, one of the leading thinkers on the topic, draws his argument for "animal liberation": "The circle of altruism has broadened from the family and tribe to the nation and race, and we are beginning to recognize that our obligations extend to all human beings. The process should not stop there."[41] Animalism sees itself as the new moral frontier to be transcended, the next criterion that will distinguish progressives from the narrow-minded. The animal species, as a criterion for demarcation and exclusion, would be just as arbitrary and oppressive as skin color or gender, and those who see good reasons for the political and moral community to remain restricted to humans would jeopardize all social gains at the same time: "we would be on shaky ground if we were to demand equality for blacks, women, and other groups of oppressed humans while denying equal consideration to nonhumans."[42] Believing that there is a single principle of equality that applies evenly to all so-called excluded groups is not self-evident, as these causes are sometimes contradictory. Nevertheless, it is a myth necessary for the smooth functioning of the intersectional coalition, which would otherwise collapse under the weight of its contradictions.

In animalist philosophy, the characterization of "speciesism" perfectly reproduces the logic of the left: It is "a foundation upon which our civilization is built,"[43] a systemic oppression that is transmitted in particular in biology classrooms, where children are taught to dissect animals, a form of systemic violence against them. Despite the overcoming of racism and sexism in Western thought, it still has a center, namely "anthropocentrism," "an approach to moral theory that takes humanity as its standard: it starts by asking what the essence is of 'being human' or 'humanity,' and assumes that human beings are entitled to rights and justice in virtue of this essential humanity."[44] Anthropocentrism, a pejorative term for humanism, is said to be a normative way of thinking and should therefore be deconstructed. The domestication of animals is its original sin, the moral equivalent of enslaving Black people, and since then, animals have been alienated in the service of humanity. The aim is therefore to advocate a new "abolitionism," deliberately borrowing the name of the American anti-slavery movement, to finally free animals from human bondage. To achieve this, nothing less than a revolution in our model of civilization would be required: "ameliorist reforms serve to legitimize, rather than contest, the system of animal enslavement, blunting what could otherwise be a more radical movement for real reform."[45] We are therefore dealing with an orthodox reading of the revolutionary matrix, whose terms are adapted to the animal condition: animals are the new proletariat, humans are the new bourgeoisie, speciesism stands in for capitalism, and the only horizon remains revolution.

For Singer, animal liberation would be the final stage of human morality, the just and equitable form of the circle of consideration. Given the constant expansion of progressive morality, he can't be too sure. "Since today's enlightened thinking often turns out to be tomorrow's hidebound conservatism . . . it would be imprudent to say too firmly that with the inclusion of non-human animals, we will at last have gone as far as impartial reasoning requires."[46] Singer leaves the door open, which some have already pushed open in anticipation of the next step in expanding the circle. To demonstrate the porosity of the boundary between humans and animals, Singer has often used the controversial comparison between animals and humans with disabilities, both in terms of their faculties and the value of their existence. This same logic can also be extrapolated to animals in a vegetative state and to plants:

> Animals that are brain dead, in a coma, or have a flat EEG are alive, and this proves that an unconscious life is possible for a being that does not have to move to survive. For the fact that roots sink into the earth and circumvent obstacles, or that leaves turn towards the sun, does not *a priori* require any more consciousness than the very fact of growing or aging. Plants are even capable of far greater feats and demonstrate a very high and complex responsiveness to their environment. But this too does not require the intervention of consciousness.[47]

Even when it seems to have reached its limit, radical exteriority finds new ways to renew itself and challenge the norm. Rationality, which excluded animals, has been replaced by consciousness, which itself becomes obsolete when we raise the issue of the suffering of non-conscious plants, left behind in a system based on consciousness, of which they would be the Other. Since accepting one inequality would mean accepting them all, stopping halfway along the path of progress becomes unthinkable, lest we fall on the conservative side and abandon the imperative of revolution. This dynamic therefore encourages the perpetual deconstruction of the norm, whatever it may be, for the benefit of supposedly excluded groups, which are constantly being renewed, and whose value is merely utilitarian in that they serve to problematize the norm and expose its alleged victims.

Excluded from Victimhood

The broadening of the criticism of civilization nevertheless creates its own margins and threatens for other groups deemed marginal what Marcuse did to the proletariat when it ceased to be the "living contradiction" of the social order. The aim is to find as revolutionary subjects those who are in the most fundamentally contradictory position in society, and not those who fit in well, or who become "upstarts" complicit with the dominant order. Thus, so-called marginalized groups are only means to the revolutionary end, and the "betrayal" of formerly marginalized groups will lead to their exclusion from the circle of the excluded, and their subsequent problematization. This mechanism of breaking solidarity on the left is the result of a marginalizing logic that moves further and further away from the norm and represents the dysfunction of the intersectional matrix. It is currently causing many groups formerly described as marginalized to lean right.

In *Où sont les femmes?*, Québécois journalist Sophie Durocher speaks out on behalf of the growing number of women who criticize the failings of the contemporary left: "The social visibility of women is shrinking like a piece of leather: it is threatened on the one hand by religious rigorism and on the other by 'inclusive' moralism. Caught between fundamentalism (which makes them disappear in the name of modesty) and wokeism (which makes them disappear in the name of concern towards marginals), women are erased, wiped out, ousted . . . and end up being forgotten."[48] As they compete with those more marginalized than themselves for the attention of critical theorists, women are losing more and more battles on the left.

This is particularly the case when their rights intersect with those of ethno-cultural minorities, especially practitioners of a strict form of Islam that is hostile to women's freedom. Consider women who are veiled to satisfy an injunction not to "arouse male desire" by letting their hair flow freely. Or the so-called "honor killings," which are anything but honorable, when a father murders his daughters because they make choices he disapproves of. It is very difficult for some feminists, who are part of the woke movement, to recognize that it is in the name of their culture and faith that the freedom, and even the lives, of these women are being violated, as Somali-born author Ayaan Hirsi Ali points out.[49]

This clash between two forms of feminism on the issue of immigration was evident in the reaction to the more than 600 rapes that took place in Cologne on December 31, 2015, at the hands of more than 1,500 asylum seekers and in the face of powerless police forces. Courageous thinkers such as French philosopher Élisabeth Badinter strongly denounced so-called intersectional feminists "who prioritized denouncing racism over protecting women."[50] Those who initially feared that this abject crime against women would be "exploited," and thus refused to denounce or publicize it, effectively demonstrated that the status of women was not their utmost priority.

The same could be said of Judith Butler, whose writings invalidate the very notion of womanhood. She asserts that "the meaning of the category remains unsettled and even enigmatic,"[51] to the point where we must "renounce the basic postulate of the subject 'woman,'"[52] which would naturally make the existence of feminism impossible. Butler is in favor of people born male competing in women's sports, even if this leads to blatant inequalities for women, because she believes that they are the more marginalized in this day and age. She also ridicules "the notion that women will feel unsafe if there is a penis in [a locker] room."[53] Yet this is precisely how many women feel, and it is neither an excessive whim nor a malicious intention. Regardless, for Butler, this critical gender feminism "is not feminism, or rather, should not be" because it "attack[s] the alliances of which feminism is an integral part, including a broader left politics."[54] Just as Marcuse discarded the proletariat, she prioritizes her political agenda over the actual rights of the women she claims to defend. The primacy now given to other causes deemed more marginal at the expense of feminism leads Sophie Durocher to assert that, while "previously, the right was the worst enemy of women," "the left is now also contributing to the decline of women's rights."[55]

October 7, 2023, and its aftermath will have shown that exclusion by the left now affects Jewish people. In the Western consciousness, Judaism has historically occupied an ambiguous position between the "Other" and the same:[56] as much as it has contributed significantly to the building of Judeo-Christian civilization, its minority position has exposed it to persecution throughout the centuries. The old anti-Semitism, that of the "deicide people" and the Elders of Zion, which culminated in the Third Reich, stigmatized it as "Other." The new anti-Semitism, which is growing on the left, attacks Jews as a Western people and stems from a decolonial ideology that projects its hatred of civilization onto them. Should we be surprised that this new "socialism of fools," as the expression goes, has its roots in Soviet socialism? In *Israelophobia*, British journalist Jake Wallis Simons points out that the demonization of the just cause of Zionism owes much to Soviet propaganda during the Cold War. In order to destabilize an ally of the United States, secure the loyalty of Arab regimes under its tutelage, and turn far-left intellectuals against the West, the USSR launched propaganda targeting Israel as a "colonial" state:

> In the minds of millions around the world, Soviet agitprop succeeded in redefining Zionism from an answer to millennia of persecution to a bourgeois, imperialist project. In this way, it wiped antisemitism clean, allowing progressives to indulge an old hatred by convincing themselves that they were merely taking a principled stand against Israel.[57]

The left's moral failure on the Jewish question continued with Michel Foucault's enthusiastic reaction to the Iranian revolution. The eternal critic of power and religion, the slayer of the panopticon and herald of insubordination, nevertheless knelt before Ayatollah Khomeini, whom he described as a "saint," a "destitute exile," a "man . . . acclaimed by his people." While he considered Christianity to be the opium of the people, he saw theocratic Islam as "the spirit of a spiritless world." To his amazement, the radical revolution sweeping across Iran became "perhaps the first great insurrection against worldly systems, the most modern form of revolt and also the craziest."[58] Because he considered the enemy of his enemy to be his friend, Foucault thus became an apologist for one of the most reactionary regimes in the world. While the traditional center-left has long stayed away from this drift, it must be acknowledged that the new radical left does not have the same reservations.

In France, Jean-Luc Mélenchon immediately springs to mind. Particularly since the 2022 presidential election and the attacks of October 7, the leader of La France Insoumise has been taking increasingly strong positions on the Israel-Palestine conflict, sometimes even against French Jews. By accusing Yaël Braun-Pivet, the Jewish speaker of the National Assembly, of "camping out in Tel Aviv to encourage the massacre"[59] and likening the CRIF, France's leading Jewish advocacy organization, to the far right,[60] he embodies the left's new hostility toward Judaism. Under Jeremy Corbyn, a long-time anti-Israel activist, the British Labour Party has become mired in similar waters. The party has been criticized by the UK Equality and Human Rights Commission for its tolerance of anti-Semitism within its ranks.[61] On the eve of the 2019 British election, the Chief Rabbi of the United Kingdom even took up his pen to assert that Labour "can no longer claim to be the party of equality and anti-racism"[62] because of its treatment of Jews. This is part of a growing trend among the radical left, which has excluded Jews from the category of "victims" it deems worthy of defending.

Due to the left's complacency toward anti-Semitism, particularly since October 7, we find figures such as Bernard-Henri Lévy lamenting that Israel would now be "alone," as if there were no salvation outside of progressivism, and especially not among "those new friends on the extreme right (*sic*) of the Western political spectrum, many of whom are reaching out to the anti-Semites."[63] For Lévy, a dyed-in the-wool progressive, it is better to be alone than allied with the right. However, intellectuals such as Yoram Hazony, author of *The Virtue of Nationalism* and a leading figure in the national-conservative movement in the Anglosphere, conclude on the contrary that "the moral outrage that has long taken aim at Israel has turned against the United States, against Britain after its vote to leave Europe, and against the nations of Eastern Europe . . . that resist European standards of behavior on a number of fronts." In other words, the hatred of Zionism expressed today targets Israelis because they "continue to act as an independent nation-state, pursuing their interests and aspirations according to their own understanding."[64] It is because Israel ostentatiously embodies the Western ideal of the nation-state against the injunctions of supranationalism and multiculturalism, and because it carries our civilizational values in the inhospitable context of the Middle East, that it attracts such harsh criticism. This is also why more and more Jews are finding that they belong more in the conservative camp in our era and that they can identify with the defense of the Judeo-Christian heritage.

To the surprise of many, a third group is increasingly distancing itself from the progressive "identity synthesis," as Yascha Mounk calls it. Citizens with immigrant backgrounds, even those who arrived relatively recently, are less and less unanimous in their support for left-wing parties, which nevertheless claim to be their most ardent defenders. The surprise was huge in the 2024 US election, when Donald Trump won no less than 43 percent of the Latino vote and 16 percent of the Black vote, an unprecedented performance for the Republican Party.[65] These results run counter to the orthodoxy that has been in vogue since the 1990s among some conservatives, according to which increased immigration would inevitably lead to an "emerging progressive majority"[66] that would politically lock in the issue of identity and migration. In the United States, many Republicans were concerned that criticism of immigration could "shade easily into bigotry," which no political party could afford because it could "cost them the growing Hispanic vote."[67] In Canada, the home of multiculturalism, this position was hegemonic within the Conservative Party, where many observers claimed that the debate on immigration was already closed, that "tolerance towards immigrants is mandated by the simple fact that there are so many of them."[68] Although it is a core belief for some, this attempt to endorse multiculturalism on the right has mainly been presented as an inevitable, rational conclusion:

> Immigrants preserve pro-immigration policies by voting for politicians who support these policies. And there are now so many immigrants that they can swing elections . . . Obviously, we believe policies of high immigration and multicultural diversity are tremendously good for Canada. But whether for good or for ill, they are entrenched and unstoppable.[69]

Yet conservative parties are becoming increasingly critical of immigration and are achieving higher scores among cultural minorities than they ever did when they repeated the progressive discourse on identity. How can we explain this counterintuitive outcome? Looking at the American case, three factors seem to be at play. First, the cultural proximity between a significant portion of immigrants and the so-called "native" nation. In *Whiteshift*, Eric Kaufmann looks back to the assimilation of those once referred to as *white ethnics*, namely Poles, Italians, and Irish, into the Anglo-Protestant American majority, whose boundaries were thus redefined. The same phenomenon seems to be at work today with Latin Americans, whose Christian culture is already very close to that of white Americans.[70] Second, the economic integration of long-time immigrants is gradually bringing them closer to the middle class and leading to a convergence of interests. Many second- or third-generation immigrants take full advantage of meritocracy and therefore do not feel economically alienated from their host country: a citizen of mixed origin who earns a middle-class salary will no longer want to vote for a party that will increase taxes and social benefits if he is the one who pays the price. Their view of immigration even changes as a result, as they identify more with the national interest: the success of Republican ads promising to close the border, broadcast in Spanish, attests to this.[71]

Ultimately, the element that alienates ethnic minorities the most from the political left comes from its own discourse: wokeism, while now ubiquitous in elite circles, does not convince anyone outside the segment of the population that invented it, namely white college graduates. American pollster Patrick Ruffini has measured this: the vast majority of citizens, across all ethnic groups, are moderate and generally lean left on economic issues and right on identity and societal issues. Only one segment of the population is predominantly highly ideological (embracing all the positions of "their side") and polarized, particularly on identity issues: white people with a university education. This creates a major difficulty for the contemporary left: unlike the right, whose vast majority of voters are rather conservative on moral issues, it has become a coalition between a hyper-progressive and almost exclusively white elite and minority voters who do not share its radical agenda.[72] This is the great unforeseen consequence of the intersectional coalition, which planned to rebuild the left without the national middle classes: even minorities no longer follow its elitist drift.

What Remains of the Left without Its Revolutionary Subject?

Once stripped of the popular aspirations it once carried and engaged in a process of systematic exclusion in which it retreats to the most radical margins, what's left of the left? It still has its true revolutionary subject, which is neither the people nor the marginalized, as Raymond Aron perceived long ago:

> Who reminds workers of their destiny? Who remains conscious of the historical mission of the proletariat against the temptations of gentrification? Intellectuals. A doctrine of intellectuals, Marxism appeals to intellectuals because of the historical role it assigns them, which elevates them in their own eyes. Intellectuals go to the proletariat to guide it, not to learn from it.[73]

Behind the intellectual's supposedly disinterested considerations lies the truth: the real class that needs to be brought to power, the one that has always been at the center of the left-wing imagination, is neither the proletariat nor its countless substitutes that have been parading since the 1960s, but the progressive intellectuals themselves. The big implication that remains the same in every adaptation of their systemic thinking is that they are the class best suited to lead, the only people who know how to do so with the necessary vision, because they are committed to "social justice." Today, wokeism is the mode of expression of a new elite, defined above all by its university degrees from prestigious institutions. Through a hermetic language, whose codes it masters in the manner of the "high culture" of yesterday's aristocracy, this elite knows how to recognize its own:

those who can chat about "cisnormativity" or "systemic racism" prove that they possess the cultural capital necessary to gain access to exclusive circles, from which "deplorables" are excluded.[74]

Moreover, by conferring on progressive intellectuals the role of a providential class, this discourse obscures the fact that elite universities are now the greatest producers of inequality in the West and that the most significant political divide has become that between university graduates and non-graduates. Thanks to the subterfuge of systemic and cultural discrimination, which is elusively embedded in national customs, this elite can cast the majority, who are less fortunate and privileged than they are, in the role of "oppressors" to be fought against.[75] A product of counterculture, it asserts its privileged social status "through delegitimizing and denigrating the institutions, traditions, values, and ways of life associated with the middle class."[76] Behind the identity debate and wokeism, therefore, lies a new class struggle, with the tables turned, between a progressive elite and the conservative middle classes.

Le Sens du peuple, French socialist Laurent Bouvet's eulogy to the old left, concludes with a Cornelian dilemma. If the working classes have swung to the right and the left is supposed to defend them, can it still exist? "The left without the people can certainly no longer exist, but the left with the people, at least this people, can no longer be the left."[77] Now that the struggle between the proletariat and the bourgeoisie no longer exists and left-wing parties have become the political vehicles of the academic elite, does the very concept of "the left" retain any meaning?

CHAPTER 5

Culture Wars Are Class Wars

IF CRITICISM OF THE West has become institutionalized, it is primarily due to sociological factors: a new progressive elite, defined by its credentials, has replaced the old bourgeois elite, which owed its status to its economic success. This seismic shift in the organization of our societies is behind the current political realignment. The naturally conservative middle class is undermined by the emergence of this new elite class and a polarization of the economy from which it suffers badly. Christopher Lasch understood the essence of this issue thirty years ago in *The Revolt of the Elites*: "The culture wars that have convulsed America since the sixties are best understood as a form of class warfare."[1] This analytical framework provides the best understanding of the rise of populism and the realignment of the divide between left and right.

The Managerial and Academic Revolution

With the industrial revolution came the emergence of the wealthy industrialist, powerful because he owned what Marx called the means of production. In the United States, these were the Rockefellers, Carnegies, and Vanderbilts, for example. Adored by some and hated by others, these big bosses acted as the ruling class, and their tension with the working class was at the heart of the classical model of class struggle between the bourgeoisie and the proletariat. However, as early as 1941, American political scientist James Burnham, author of *The Managerial Revolution*, announced the end of the reign of big bosses. For this reformed communist, who became a CIA operative, the advent of the welfare state and, with it, a new class of managers sounded the death knell for the old industrial elite, which had been overtaken by a power greater than its own:

> The managers will exercise their control over the instruments of production and gain preference in the distribution of the products, not directly, through property rights vested in them as individuals, but indirectly, through their control of the state which will in turn own and control the instruments of production. The state—that is, the institutions which comprise the state—will be, if we wish to put it that way, the "property" of *the* managers. And that will be quite enough to place them in the position of the ruling class.[2]

Whereas in the past, personal ownership of the means of production was the ultimate guarantee of power, the managerial revolution of the mid-century led to a "separation of ownership and control,"[3] which deprived the big capitalists of a considerable part of their political power. Rather than material success, it is now higher education, expanded in the aftermath of World War II, that serves as the breeding ground for elites. French sociologist Emmanuel Todd has quantified this higher education revolution: in 1900, only 3 percent of men and 2 percent of women had the equivalent of a bachelor's degree, while this proportion gradually reached 27 percent and 22.5 percent in 1975, before stabilizing at around one-third of the population in the twenty-first century.[4] As more and more students join the ranks of universities and the industries that employ university graduates account for a growing share of GDP, the institution gains power, to the point of exercising a monopoly over the designation of individuals who can attain senior positions within the state or big corporations. A stratification process takes hold within these institutions, as only a handful of them offer (or deny) privileged social status and entry into elite circles. These are the French Grandes Écoles, the American Ivy League, and the British Russell Group, for example.

At the same time, the meaning of higher education is changing: "People no longer pursue higher education to gain independence. We pursue higher education to reach the top of the social pyramid if we are ambitious, to remain there if we are from a wealthy family, or to avoid downward mobility if we are from a modest background."[5] This explains the phenomenon of "credential inflation," whereby jobs that previously required a bachelor's degree now require a master's degree: if university serves primarily to establish a hierarchy, then the relative generalization of a degree level requires ambitious individuals to outbid each other with even higher degrees, according to Michael Lind, who refers to the equivalent of a "credential arms race" to maintain an advantage in the market.[6]

Higher education today therefore has little to do with the emancipatory ideal of education, that of the individual cultivating themselves for personal fulfillment. Instead, it is a kind of Faustian bargain, requiring people to spend more and more time in a bubble disconnected from society at large, exempt from both the rules of childhood and the responsibilities of adulthood, and to delay entering the labor market and starting a family in exchange for the promise of a place at the top of the social ladder. In the words of Christopher Lasch, "a migratory way of life is the price of getting ahead," while "those who stay at home forfeit the chance of upward mobility."[7] Globalization and the falling cost of transport and communications have also intensified the uprooting required of students: whereas in the past, leaving one's province for a regional metropolis such as Montreal or Chicago was more than enough, professional opportunities are now more centralized than ever in a few select cities, such as New York, London, or Toronto. This new elite is thus fundamentally different from "the old-money ethic of civic responsibility,"[8] because the power of the latter depended on their roots in a local community and their contribution to the good of that community, unlike the mobility that characterizes managerial elites.

The geographical uprooting of elite education is also accompanied by prolonged immersion in an ideological monoculture, particularly in the humanities. According to a survey by Professor Eric Kaufmann, 83 percent of professors in American humanities departments would vote for the left, compared to 82 percent in the United Kingdom and 73 percent in Canada. In comparison, only 6 percent of American professors surveyed identify as right-wing, compared to 14 percent of British professors and 7 percent of Canadian professors.[9] These proportions are in no way representative of society as a whole, but it is nevertheless in this closed environment that the future Western elites must immerse themselves, leading to a predictable disconnect with the general population. What's more, a real ideological intolerance is emerging on the left, with progressive graduates more reluctant to socialize with or even hire someone who votes for the right, while the reverse is not true.[10] One need only look at how woke thinkers talk about those who oppose their project. Judith Butler laments that her critics "do not read books in gender or feminist studies, queer or trans studies, queer of color critique, Black feminism, or any version of race theory" and assumes that this lack of interest stems from a position that "refuses questions, challenges, and a spirit of open inquiry," a "fear that intellectual debates may well confuse them about the values they hold." Since it is impossible "to make [their] enemies smarter," they should simply be ignored.[11]

A Countercultural Elite

The managerial and academic revolution has thus brought about a radical change in the nature of Western elites, as diagnosed by several essays published at the turn of the twenty-first century. As Richard Florida theorizes a "creative class" and Musa Al-Gharbi speaks of "symbolic capitalists," David Brooks refers instead to bourgeois bohemians, the famous "bobos,"[12] to describe this new elite, whose ideology is the product of its disconnection from productive work, of a life in "an artificial environment from which everything that resists human control (unavoidably, everything familiar and reassuring as well) has been rigorously excluded."[13] This shift from conservatism to progressivism at the top of society is nothing less than a social and political earthquake:

> The Creative Class is the norm-setting class of our time. And the norms of the Creative Class are different from those of more traditional society. Individuality, self-expression, and openness to difference are valued over the homogeneity, conformity, and "fitting in" that defined the previous era of large-scale industry and organization.[14]

The new elite is defined by its degrees and beliefs rather than its material wealth: It is the product of university towns and globalized metropolises, which share a social and cultural composition very different from rural regions: "It has to be diverse. It has to have a visible gay community; it has to have lots of different races and ethnic groups. It has to have people of all ages and be open to young people. It has to have people who *look* different."[15] The countercultural elite, which explicitly rebelled against the standardized image of the 1950s middle class and its normalizing conformism, seeks exactly the opposite, valuing above all eccentricity and "difference." While a famous study by Robert Putnam asserts that ethno-cultural pluralism reduces "social capital" in a community and leads to its members becoming more inward-looking,[16] Richard Florida counters with the "creative capital" of globalized cities, which is inversely proportional to social capital but predicts economic development and the concentration of skilled professionals in our age.[17]

The shift toward a countercultural, educated elite has also led to a different mechanism for the reproduction of elites. While aristocracy was hereditary and capitalism celebrated entrepreneurial success, the power of the bourgeois bohemians depends on a "pluralistic meritocracy,"[18] which prides itself on being open to marginalized identities, while remaining very closed in terms of the type of profiles it values, namely university graduates, all from what David Goodhart calls the "cognitive class," as opposed to manual laborers or "heart" workers, who populate sectors such as health care, social work, and primary and secondary education.[19] The creative class has inherited the greatest flaw of meritocracy, namely the belief that anyone who does not reach the top of the pyramid is undeserving,[20] and therefore intellectually and morally inferior. Their tolerance toward foreigners and marginalized groups goes hand in hand with "intolerance for [the] mediocrity" of ordinary people.[21] Progressive values therefore serve as a test of whether or not one belongs to the ruling class:[22] those who reject them will simultaneously lose their privileged status, regardless of their qualifications. The American practice of requiring a "diversity statement"[23] signed by job or university applicants reveals this naked bias: anyone who does not share the elite values of "diversity, equity, and inclusion" is not welcome. Since this class sees itself as the sole holder of knowledge, those who disagree with it can only be wrong: either they are intolerant (racist, homophobic, transphobic, etc.), or they lack education and information, and therefore do not deserve to be listened to.[24]

The new elite has a class consciousness: it feels trapped and frustrated in the ruins of the old world of Western traditions[25] and wants to live with its own kind in a new world that matches its aspirations. This is why economic success is not its ultimate priority. When given the choice between the fate of a wealthy worker or that of a poor "creative," it opts for the latter, because it perceives its social status as its most precious asset.[26] Is it any wonder, then, that the new progressive elite's worst enemies come from the ranks of entrepreneurial success, such as dropout entrepreneur Elon Musk and real estate developer Donald Trump? Despite their personal fortunes, such figures can never feel like full members of this new elite, because their path to success belongs to that of the old economic elite, pushed from its pedestal by the managerial revolution.

Driven by the illusion of meritocracy, the new academic elite is convinced that its dominance is legitimate, natural, and unquestionable. What's more, it has hegemonic ambitions and wants to continue its expansion toward the "*creatification* of everyone."[27] Following the example of Tony Blair, who dreamed of sending 50 percent of young Britons to university,[28] degrees are increasingly required for white-collar jobs that did not require them in the past, such as journalists and political advisors, but also for blue-collar or "pink-collar" jobs, such as police officers and nurses.[29] Graduates are also capturing civil society, as associations that once relied on the voluntary work of large numbers of people from all walks of life are becoming professionalized NGOs, run by a small number of members of the cognitive class.[30] Living amongst themselves, the new elites come to believe that they represent the entire democratic body and that they alone are essential for the functioning of Western societies. However, as this class grows, it creates an increasingly hierarchical society that is far removed from the middle class shaped by the New Deal era.

The De-Middle-Classification of the West

According to pollster Jérôme Fourquet, in the postwar years, "most of the working classes and lower middle classes became fully integrated into French society," creating at the same time "a vast central body, bringing together . . . two out of three French people."[31] This strong middle class, which emerged throughout the West, is naturally conservative in its values because, unlike the creative class, which identifies with an eccentric minority, it identifies above all with the nation and the figure of the majority.[32] One could even say that what defines the middle class, before its economic status, is precisely this identification with the majority figure. Having middle-class values therefore means being more patriotic than individualistic, respecting established rules and customs, and valuing the traditional family and law enforcement agencies such as the police and the military.[33] It is indeed logical that people who set the norm because of their economic and cultural status identify with it and are therefore less inclined to defend individuality and eccentricity, which challenge their own way of life. Historically, according to historian David Stebenne, the most characteristic policies of the middle class have been economic protectionism, low immigration, and a substantial social safety net,[34] which resembles what most Western populists defend today.

The middle class is also an important vehicle for integration: immigrants who are economically successful and join the American middle class tend to vote more like the majority than like minorities.[35] While it acts as a melting pot for integration into the nation, it also constitutes the indispensable foundation of a strong democracy and has done so since Athens.[36] Indeed, it becomes difficult to accept majority rule, the first principle of democracy, if one does not belong to the general will that it is supposed to express. Conversely, anyone who identifies with the polity is much more likely to accept its verdict, even when it does not reflect their personal preferences. Compared to the middle class, classes that do not fully identify with the nation have always been the most resistant to its normative values. During the New Deal era, big business and the African American minority (which suffered from racial segregation) were the two main sources of opposition to Franklin Roosevelt's public works policy, which provided jobs for what would become the American middle class.[37] For the same reason, elites and non-integrated minorities are less inclined toward patriotism, which implies adherence to a norm in which they find themselves less materially or culturally than the majority middle class,[38] due to the link between normality in the numerical sense and normativity as an ideal to aspire to.

The revolution in mass higher education, the relocation of many blue-collar jobs to non-Western countries, and the significant rise in immigration in recent decades have reversed the trend of economic and cultural convergence that characterized the postwar economic boom. Fourquet refers to a "de-averaging," but one could also theorize a polarization between a graduate elite and a lumpenproletariat that is economically and culturally unintegrated, two blocs that are gaining ground at the expense of the national middle class and its values. In the words of Emmanuel Todd, "the development of higher education has broken the cultural homogeneity of the social body, which, since the mid-1960s, can be described as stratified, ripe for economic inequality."[39] Some even theorize a return to feudalism, or a hyper-hierarchical caste society like the one that prevailed in the Middle Ages, before the advent of democracy.[40] This polarization is a product of the hollowing out of the industrial economy and the decline of blue-collar jobs, which for a long time were the backbone of the middle class. On the contrary, in an economy dominated by the creative class, it is in the low-cost service sector that demand for labor is exploding:

> As the economy has become more specialized and the occupational division of labor has deepened, the Creative Class has increasingly outsourced functions that were previously provided within the family to the Service Class . . . A few entrepreneurially minded members may be successful enough to open their own restaurants, lawn and garden services, for example. But many have no way out; they are stuck for life in menial jobs.[41]

It seems that those who applauded the rise of the service sector have forgotten that there are far more McDonald's cashiers, Amazon delivery drivers, and Uber drivers than Goldman Sachs bankers in the service economy. This new polarized economy is that of today's major cities: a highly educated, predominantly white elite who do not have children until they are thirty (if they decide to have them at all), and a very poorly paid and largely immigrant underclass.[42] These metropolises aim to become "premier global destination[s] and hub[s] for highly educated, entrepreneurial people,"[43] cities that combine tolerance for diversity with intolerance for "mediocrity," according to the new elite's values.

The industries that define this new economic model also operate in a polarized manner. At universities, permanent faculty can count on an army of poorly paid lecturers whose only dream is to one day obtain a professorship. On social media, a handful of influencers and "content creators" get all the attention, while the rest are reduced to the status of spectators. Service giants such as Uber and Amazon hire a handful of programmers for an army of delivery drivers and chauffeurs who often earn little more than minimum wage. It is no coincidence that the idea of a guaranteed minimum income is increasingly resurfacing in elite circles. If work is no longer sufficiently remunerative for the servants of the creative class, it will have to agree to grant them enhanced benefits to help them make ends meet. Thus, with the exodus of manufacturing jobs and the growth of the service sector driven by the educated elite, wealth gaps have narrowed between countries, but have widened with inside Western countries.[44] It should also be noted that the importation of low-cost immigrant labor is essentially a reverse form of offshoring: rather than exporting factories where workers accept lower wages, workers who are willing to work for less are imported into Western countries.

This upheaval in the very structure of society has given rise to a new class struggle, which no longer has anything to do with the conflict between the bourgeoisie and the proletariat theorized in Marx's writings. Michael Lind, author of *The New Class War*, echoes Christopher Lasch's observation in describing a class struggle that does not say its name behind the identity politics that are now front and center all over the West.[45] While David Brooks predicted that the supremacy of the bourgeois bohemians would not be threatened in the short or medium term, because pluralistic meritocracy would ensure its reproduction by co-opting the "best" regardless of their origin,[46] he overlooked the national middle classes, which now constitute the largest source of opposition to the metropolitan economic alliance between the creative class and low-wage immigrant workers.

The often-criticized gentrification of cities would be better described as bipolarization: the real estate market is dominated by luxury condos for childless bobos or by public housing towers to accommodate the service class, which cannot afford to live there but which the creative class needs to keep close by. The middle classes, on the other hand, are pushed out to the suburbs, the last refuge for those who want to own a single-family home and raise children.[47] At the same time, they are made invisible and excluded from culture, advertising, boards of directors, and all those intermediary bodies where the "representativeness" touted by the new elite implies a passage through pluralistic and academic meritocracy. As its normative status, essential to its understanding of itself as middle class, is marginalized, the national middle class feels that it simply does not belong in the world shaped by the creative class.

The Decline of Civil Society

According to Alexis de Tocqueville's pluralist vision, intermediary bodies and other associations are necessary "to prevent the despotism of faction or the arbitrary power of a prince." They are democratic institutions that "are formed and maintained by the agency of private individuals" and are therefore representative of the multiplicity of views and interests that make up society.[48] However, with the decline in social and community participation, as documented by Robert Putnam in *Bowling Alone*,[49] associations have become professionalized and are now run by paid activists from academia,[50] rather than by average citizens in their spare time. This major change completely reverses the role of associations: rather than being the voice of groups ignored in public debate, they become yet another mouthpiece for the elite class, which explains why most NGOs broadly defend the same worldview. Amnesty International, Oxfam, and the American Civil Liberties Union, for example, rarely disagree, to the point that they have become inseparable, as if they were the spokespersons for the same political party rather than representatives of a diversity of viewpoints, as Tocqueville would have wished. However, the state finances most of their budget through subsidies or tax exemptions on donations, thereby endorsing the stranglehold of one class, and one political camp, on the public debate.[51] Outside of the United States, the conservative movement has no institutions comparable in size and resources.

The doctrine of separation of powers, dear to thinkers of democracy, has also declined with the rise in importance of administrative power, a result of the growth of the welfare state and the increasing complexity of laws. Max Weber envisioned a permanent and neutral bureaucracy, appointed on the basis of competence rather than arbitrariness, which would therefore serve any government elected by the people to the best of its ability. However, this ideal of administrative independence has degenerated into a technocratic power that too often seeks to be independent of the will of the elected government, acting as a replacement rather than an auxiliary to the will of the people.[52] The setbacks of the last British Conservative government attest to this: several ministers have publicly stated that they encountered significant resistance within the state to implementing Brexit, due to a civil service strongly committed to remaining in the European Union.[53] Disagreeing with Rishi Sunak's plan to deport illegal migrants to Rwanda, the civil service union even took the government to court (unsuccessfully) to avoid having to implement it.[54] In this context, it surprised no one that a civil servant would openly celebrate the victory of Keir Starmer's Labour Party in *The Guardian*.[55]

When the cognitive class today evokes the separation of powers, it often has in mind the protection of its own power within public institutions in the face of opposing political will, guided by what it perceives as the "base instincts" of the people.[56] Since it sees itself as embodying "reason," it does not need countervailing powers to curb its excesses: by its very existence, it *is* the countervailing power against the ignorance and prejudices of its less "enlightened" fellow citizens.[57] Nevertheless, it is not uncommon for politicians themselves to play this role by claiming to want to "depoliticize" contentious debates, such as the one on medical assistance in dying,[58] which in practical terms means removing them from democratic debate in favor of a predetermined outcome based on the preferences of the managerial class. The tendency to praise "depoliticization," a concept that seems to enjoy an aura of sanctity, enshrines the rise in influence of unelected individuals who generally share the same opinions, to the detriment of the only power over which citizens exercise control, the elected government. In a representative democracy where popular power is delegated to elected officials, we should be concerned when they in turn delegate it on a massive scale.

Even when elected officials play their role and vote on laws, it is not uncommon for the judiciary to intervene, censoring or completely rewriting the will of the legislature. In the United States and Canada, where a highly activist system of judicial review prevails, the doctrine of the "living Constitution," as opposed to strict adherence to the original intent of the Fathers of Confederation, amounts to a license for unbridled activism, bound only by the wishes of the judges who engage in it. For example, when the US Civil Rights Act was passed in 1964, Congress explicitly stated in the law that it could not be interpreted to sanction "reverse" discrimination on the basis of race, with one senator even assuring that if this were the case, he would eat the pages of the law himself.[59] However, the Supreme Court interpreted the law differently, arguing that although explicit quotas were prohibited, discrimination on the basis of ethnicity was acceptable in the interest of a "diverse" student body,[60] marking the beginning of the overused concept of "diversity" in institutions. In the same fashion, the French Constitutional Council's censorship of a considerable number of articles in the Immigration Law passed in 2023[61] calls into question the real power now conferred on elected officials to tackle an issue such as immigration, on which the majority has clear expectations for reduction, repeatedly expressed but rarely implemented.

After decades of transferring power from elected officials to administrations and the judiciary in a process of "fragmentation of norm-setting bodies,"[62] the political activism of big business, sometimes referred to as "woke capitalism," seems more like a culmination than a break with the past. One of its first manifestations came in 2016, when North Carolina passed a law requiring individuals to use public restrooms corresponding to their birth gender, and sixty-eight companies, including giants such as Apple and eBay, subsequently sued the state on behalf of the transgender cause.[63] Before the managerial revolution, when it was still believed that the main role of a company was to sell a product or service in order to make a profit, big bosses would never have gotten directly involved, on behalf of their companies, in a political debate that had nothing to do with their business. As a result of the capture of institutions by an ideologically homogeneous class, it is not laws that compel companies to act in this way, but "a form of implicit agreement on the new values that characterize our society,"[64] "the violation of which is certainly not punishable by law but can destroy a company's reputation in a matter of hours."[65] In a relatively closed environment, populated by graduates who have been fed the same ideas, there is no need to formally prohibit certain comments or positions; everyone knows exactly what they can and cannot say in order to walk the line. Unsurprisingly, it is employees whose beliefs are "contrary to those conveyed by their company and the current climate"[66] who are afraid to take a political stance. Rather than acting as guardians of a democratic and pluralistic society, the most vocal intermediary bodies, whether universities, companies, NGOs, or even "independent" state bodies, have become mouthpieces for progressive thinking. Laurent Bouvet goes so far as to say that civil society "is taking . . . the place of the people as the political and social collective of reference"[67] on the left.

This sociological and political shift poses an unprecedented challenge to right-wing political theory. While the Cold War and the fight against socialist revolution had accustomed conservatism to defending the liberal bourgeoisie against the people, suspected of being revolutionary, the revolt of the elites and their shift to the progressive camp structurally disrupted its conception of democracy.[68] It therefore ceased to view political struggle according to the liberal model, in a two-term equation that pits the state against the citizen, in favor of a three-player model: the state, civil society institutions, and the people. When intermediary bodies cease to be representative, abuse their power, or act against the interests of the majority, as was the case following the revolt of the elites, it is incumbent upon the state to assert itself in order to ensure the common good and respect for the democratic majority.[69] This vision of politics is an old one, dating back to Machiavelli's *Discourses on Livy*.[70] This philosophical shift forms the basis of contemporary populist doctrine, that of a right wing that has shed its old elitist ways to defend the people, who have become the most conservative component of the social order in the West. It thus blurs the lines with what was until yesterday the preserve of the left.

CHAPTER 6

Populism's Rights and Wrongs

POPULISM AS A POLITICAL concept is notoriously difficult to define, to the point where many have given up on attributing any specific ideological content to it. For German political scientist Jan-Werner Müller, it is primarily a rhetorical framework that pits the people against the elites, with one side claiming a moral monopoly on representation: "Populists claim that they, and they alone, represent the people."[1] The populist shift within the Western right nevertheless represents a particular philosophical synthesis, offering a response to the alignment between "culture wars" and class struggle. While it has so far managed to rack up victories, both political and cultural, and to bring fundamental issues such as national identity, immigration, and the condition of the middle classes back to the forefront of public debate, it is not immune to temptations as destructive as the progressivism it opposes.

Conservatives Who Speak like Marxists?

At the heart of populism's ideology lies the breakdown of the founding synthesis of the postwar political right, namely the alliance of convenience between classical liberalism and a form of conservatism focused on protecting customs and traditions. The American thinker Frank Meyer called this "fusionism," a coalition cemented in the fight against totalitarianism, especially the communist threat from Moscow.[2] This agreement lasted for several decades because both wings of the right-wing coalition were aware of the urgent need to defeat communism, which threatened both freedoms and traditions. After the fall of the Berlin Wall, the two sensibilities gradually drifted apart, reaching a breaking point with the emergence of the civilizational question. Freedom and virtue do not always go hand in hand, and issues related to morals and national identity tend to systematically divide them. While conservatives lament the breakdown of the traditional family, increased immigration, and the erosion of cultural transmission between generations, many classical liberals view these harmful trends as results of individual choices, or increased prosperity, that cannot be called into question.[3]

Faced with this fundamental divergence, populists such as J. D. Vance conclude, "The old conservative movement argued if you just got government out of the way, natural forces would resolve problems—we are no longer in this situation and must take a different approach."[4] After making "extinguishing fires its sole objective," the right must now "fight fire with fire."[5] In other words, it is not enough to oppose the project promoted by the left and to remain entrenched in a primitive aversion to state power. On the contrary, the right must propose its own vision of the good and embody it in its governance. This change of course also marks the end of the elitism that traditionally prevailed on the right. In the era of the *Revolt of the Elites*, conservatives have no use for Ortega y Gasset's framework of the *Revolt of the Masses*:

> The mass is that part which does not act of itself. Such is its mission. It has come into the world in order to be directed, influenced, represented, organized—even in order to cease being mass, or at least to aspire to this. But it has not come into the world to do all this by itself. It needs to submit its life to a higher court, formed of the superior minorities.[6]

After the managerial revolution and the emergence of progressive elites, this position would be completely anachronistic on the right. Parties that are too institutional, whose discourse has not changed in this regard, are paying the price today, while conservatism has gradually appropriated the grievances of the "white trash," the "rednecks," and other "deplorables," the scapegoats of the new world. This resemblance is not accidental: In many ways, populist discourse often looks like the right has adopted the language of the left and reformulated its demands through the prism of victimhood culture, perhaps the only way to be heard these days.

French geographer Christophe Guilluy has written extensively on this invisible and forgotten "peripheral France" where the majority of the population actually lives, and recounts the misery of the working classes, caught up in the anxiety of social decline. Following Donald Trump's victory in 2016, the economic decline of "poor whites" due to globalization was the dominant framework for explaining the support of former working-class Democrats to the Republican candidate. The right did not distance itself from this narrative, since Trump gave it a moral veneer, which it had not had for a long time. J. D. Vance, now vice president of the United States, became a national figure thanks to his autobiography *Hillbilly Elegy*, which recounts the suffering of "poor whites" in Appalachia, described as the last class it is now permissible to despise, a class devoid of heroes because it has been forbidden to have them.[7] Marine Le Pen, who has long echoed the grievances of the "losers of globalization," also frequently plays the card of defender of the "little people" against the "establishment," which has contributed to making her more acceptable in public opinion.

Thus, even the most vocal critics of victimhood culture can adopt its moral framework,[8] which Jonathan Haidt calls the dichotomy between care and suffering.[9] Overused by the left and long neglected by the right, this appeal to emotion consists of eliciting sympathy by listing the difficulties and miseries faced by a group. Some, like Guilluy, find it humiliating for the working classes to flaunt their misfortunes in this way.[10] The fact remains that the most politically acceptable way to challenge the new orthodoxy, which claims to speak on behalf of the excluded and marginalized, is to talk about the people it "really" excludes, whom the left has ostracized for half a century. First among them are the "losers of globalization," who have been weakened by the political choices of the academic class. The triumph of the culture of victimization is so complete, notes French journalist Eugénie Bastié, that all political sides now claim to be losing the war of ideas in order to elicit sympathy and place themselves in the position of the underdog: "A major feature of contemporary intellectual debate is that each faction wants to claim to be a minority and oppressed by the others."[11] Doesn't it show how hegemonic counterculture has become, when everyone wants to be seen as a dissident?

The Rise of a Conservative Left

This rhetorical reversal has attracted new allies to the conservative side, defectors from the left who will forever claim: "I am left-wing, I have always been left-wing, I will always be left-wing, and yet I do not recognize myself, or only very little, in the fifty shades of red now available on the market of ideas."[12] At least since the nineteenth century, a "conservative left" has existed in the intellectual world, although it has never truly identified with a political party. Today, it is associated with thinkers such as Christopher Lasch and George Orwell in the Anglosphere, although it is much more prominent in France. In many ways, these figures from the ranks of the left are the organic intellectuals of conservative populism today, as the right has appropriated many of their observations.

This sensibility can be described as "the Marxist or socialist condemnation of the economic model specific to capitalism and, on the other hand, the anti-modern, anti-progressive—and sometimes even nostalgic for an old world—condemnation of the social and anthropological consequences of this same model."[13] In contemporary France, Jean-Claude Michéa is undoubtedly the purest representative of this current. His thesis of the "unity of liberalism," according to which economic liberalization and moral liberalization are two sides of the same coin, both leading to the alienation of the individual, is the basic observation shared by left-wing conservatives.[14] In France especially, a part of the left that is very attached to the republican idea, to the nation, and to *laïcité* has also broken ranks to enter into dissent with the liberal and woke left. They all share a common aversion to "a 'left' that is despised because it is considered 'liberal-libertarian' and has betrayed the fundamental principles of early socialism,"[15] namely the defense of the working classes. The institutional left is very critical of these defectors and has loudly excommunicated them since the beginning of the twenty-first century, branding them "new reactionaries."[16]

Although it usually describes itself as a "politically orphaned third party,"[17] the conservative left nevertheless has a project very similar to that of the conservatives who have embraced populism. It divides the people it defends into three distinct facets: the democratic people as a sovereign community of citizens capable of self-determination, the social people as agents of emancipation and representatives of the less fortunate classes, and the national people, embodied in a distinct cultural identity necessary for communal life.[18] A right wing that defends the aspirations of the majority, that addresses social issues from the perspective of the middle classes weakened by globalization, and that places the question of identity at the center of its discourse, meets the expectations of these three figures of the people. This project of "returning to the aspirations of the majority, and therefore to the democratic framework, [which] will lead us towards a more coherent society,"[19] as well as that of "belonging to a coherent and stable community, capable of enduring over time,"[20] also addresses the issue central to conservatives, the weakening cohesion of the social order. Bouvet was therefore extremely lucid in anticipating that "rediscovering the meaning of the people could well lead the left directly to the right."[21]

This is precisely the mockery faced by the conservative left, which is accused of camouflaging "right-wing thinking in left-wing language."[22] For older figures, such as the late socialist Jacques Julliard, the accusation is an insult, leading them to regret that "this unwavering loyalty to the values of the left is enough to make us suspect of deviating from them."[23] On the other hand, among younger people, political labels do not carry the same importance. While they "advocate a return to 'limits to resist the liberal-libertarian steamroller'" and "embrace their conservatism," they intend to "move beyond the traditional divide between right and left," a product of a bygone era that they have not really experienced.[24] It must be noted that in the contemporary conservative coalition, cemented by the populist shift, there are intellectuals and, above all, voters who come from both sides of the political spectrum, mirroring the conservative fringes of the right and left, which have each traveled their own paths to arrive at similar conclusions.

The Contrarian Temptation

While this intellectual convergence around the idea of conservatism undoubtedly represents the best of populism, it is not the only cause behind its rise. Cynicism toward the political class, and calls to "drain the swamp," contribute powerfully to it. Populism draws much of its energy, its discourse, and sometimes even its popularity from its simple opposition to the established order. In practice, its ideology often seems "clearer in what it rejects than what it wishes for."[25] The risk of such a position is that it can become bogged down in "contrarianism," or opposition on principle to dominant ideas, whatever they may be, according to political scientist Marc Crapez's definition: "Yes, I am a contrarian. I take the opposite view to conventional wisdom. As a matter of principle. Like a critical gadfly. Always contrary."[26] Yascha Mounk speaks of "180-ism," the tendency of many participants in public debate to declare themselves diametrically opposed to whatever their adversaries suggest.[27] While a certain spirit of contradiction is necessary to criticize anti-civilization, it would be a mistake to think that negation is good in itself. Ironically, this would be to reproduce the countercultural pattern, imagining oneself "alone against everyone, the only one who is not a 'sheep,' the new democratic symbol of the twenty-first century."[28] Contrarianism is a methodology, not an ideology, and turning it into a sacred cow would derail the populist movement and turn it into yet another form of nihilism.

This is the criticism that Donald Trump frequently faces. He himself embodies a countercultural figure. Behind his initial success is his tendency to deliberately violate expectations of political correctness, or even politeness, toward traditional politicians. Trump is a pure product of the ethic of authenticity, his vulgar style being perceived as more "authentic" than that of polite and civilized elected officials in an era where the self is king.[29] When we hear Trump insulting, swearing, or more generally breaking social codes one after another, no one doubts that he follows his impulses. Similarly, his discourse on fake news resembles a reversal of left-wing ideas against themselves, because postmodernism and relativism did not originate on the right.[30] If Christopher Caldwell describes the rise of the libertarian right under Reagan as a complementary continuation of the counterculture of the sixties,[31] one might be tempted to see Trump as the right-wing backlash to the woke revolution:

> What makes the alt-right a countercultural phenomenon is that it has internalized the essential feature of the counterculture: the celebration of rule-breaking or norm-violation in whatever form. What makes it a conservative phenomenon is that the rules or norms of collective action or conformity that it seeks to undermine are those championed by the left under the guise of political correctness . . . In general, whenever a norm or rule is designed to facilitate collective action in the name of progress, the alt-right sees itself as dutybound to violate it. Dissent is seen as an intrinsically political act.[32]

A fundamental question therefore arises for the populist movement: Is it a conservative movement, which aims to protect a certain idea of the West, or, on the contrary, a mere counterculture for white men? This ambivalence is not unique to Trumpism and unfortunately applies to the entire right wing, which "has historically often been satisfied with being anti-establishment, rarely able to define itself positively, sometimes turning into a party of resistance to the left, an anti-left, or yesterday's left."[33] Yet Chesterton was right to claim that "a permanent ideal is as necessary to the innovator as to the conservative" and that "reform implies form. It implies that we are trying to shape the world in a particular image; to make it something that we see already in our minds."[34] Without the nation, history, and tradition, the right cannot hope to embody the party of rootedness. At best, it will be a disoriented left, a countercultural movement that will pursue decadence, polarization, and chaos rather than curb them. At worst, it would become a conspiracy theory, an "oppositional mindset" that "cannot offer anything in place" of the system it criticizes.[35]

Particularly during the COVID pandemic, populism flirted with the temptation to cease being a conservative movement and instead represent the people in their most nihilistic form. Steve Bannon, Trump's former advisor, describes this new synthesis as "MAGA plus," or the addition of the Make America Great Again base and all those dissatisfied with the social order, primarily anti-sanitary measures activists, many of whom come from the left.[36] Naomi Klein calls this synthesis "diagonal politics," which cuts across the left and right to unite all those who are dissatisfied, all those who want to challenge the established order. What unites them is a radical skepticism toward power, as well as a particular aversion to established institutions.[37] At a time when dissatisfaction with leaders is high and mistrust is on the rise, particularly among young people,[38] there is no doubt that this temptation will cross all Western populisms, but it may well neutralize their power for genuine reform. In other words, if populism, as a counterculture, is to succeed, it must give rise to a counter-elite capable of exercising responsibility and reshaping the country in its own image:

> A counterculture defines itself in opposition to the establishment. A counterestablishment wants to be the establishment. Members of a counterculture relish their outsider status. Members of a counterestablishment regret their outsider status. A counterculture is the heckler in the audience. A counterestablishment is the understudy, waiting in the wings for a chance to play the title role.[39]

The big question facing populists today is therefore that of their professionalization, their ability to move beyond the "drain the swamp" mentality and become a new elite, capable of exercising power and truly reforming Western democracies. A modern society without elites does not exist. Elites will continue to exist as long as hierarchical structures such as the state, the university, or simply the accumulation of wealth remain. Moreover, one of the basic lessons of political action is that "a determined and focused minority can override the desires of a diffuse and unorganized majority, even a large one."[40] Rejecting elites as such would be a costly mistake as it would only prolong the crisis we are going through indefinitely, in the form of a constantly renewed confrontation between an inarticulate mass and out-of-touch leaders.

The Lie of "beyond Left and Right"

As populist discourse borrows elements from the left and unites its disillusioned supporters, the temptation to abandon its conservative foundations and simply become the "old left" will inevitably arise. There is already talk of a "double continuity" between the National Rally and the former French Communist Party, "electoral privilege among the working classes on the one hand, and stigmatization by the ruling classes on the other." French pollster and RN supporter Jérôme Sainte-Marie presents a possible victory for the RN as the return of the working classes to the political scene "for the first time since 1981,"[41] implying continuity with socialist president François Mitterrand. While this is not strictly speaking untrue from a demographic point of view, populist movements could well be enchanted by their "left-wing sociology"[42] once in power and satisfy themselves with implementing a social-democratic economic program, neglecting the cultural springboard that is inextricably linked to their rise.

This approach is already being considered by some American populist intellectuals who, although opposed to illegal immigration, propose to "enact amnesties for illegal immigrants in countries like the US where large numbers of unauthorized foreign nationals . . . are de facto citizens" as a means of "denying employers the ability to pit different groups of workers against one another."[43] The populist magazine *Compact* also analyzed the 2023 riots in French immigrant *banlieues* following the death of Nahel Merzouk in a police intervention as "bread riots," completely sidestepping the cultural issue and turning it into an economic story.[44] The "new class war" is left aside in favor of the old one, that of the socialist left. Will those who viewed populism favorably because it embodied something like a return to history or a way of saving utopianism in a world disenchanted by the victory of liberalism[45] be satisfied with its leftist rhetoric without its right-wing foundation? The National Rally is not the Workers' Rally, and its vote is not just a class vote, but most of all a patriotic and conservative vote.[46] Pollster Jérôme Fourquet notes that "social concerns are always relegated to second place among this electorate," which is primarily motivated by social and identity issues.[47] This is what separates the National Rally from the Socialist Party and the French Communist Party, and their meager scores of between 1.7 and 2.2 percent in the 2022 presidential election. Despite its rhetoric "beyond left and right," populism was born on the right as a reaction against an anti-Western left and must remain so to fulfill its promise of reform.

Beyond the sociological divide between the people and the elite, the current wave of populism in the West is based on ideological and cultural foundations. If the right has taken a populist turn, it is primarily because the ruling classes have embraced the countercultural discourse and do not seem willing to slow down the dissolution of Western nation states. British political scientist Matthew Goodwin, one of the most astute observers of the phenomenon, sees it as primarily a cultural divide between "cosmopolitans and traditionalists, between those whose values instinctively support the new elite and the revolution and those who, instead, feel far more strongly attached to the nation, the majority group, and who desperately want to find leaders who will preserve their distinctive national identity, culture and ways of life."[48] The traditionalist camp is therefore looking for elites who will defend the nation and the majority, slow the pace of social change, and encourage a certain conformity to the established way of life.

This electoral coalition has the potential to win a large majority, as demonstrated by Boris Johnson's decisive victory in 2019, as he managed to embody populist rhetoric within the institutional vehicle that is the Tory Party. Uniting pensioners, workers, and voters without degrees, he left Jeremy Corbyn's Labour Party with only the core vote of the contemporary left: young people, university graduates, and a portion of cultural minorities.[49] Johnson's 163-seat majority, which transcended social classes, proves that victory does not depend on a "politics of recognition" toward workers, but rather on a conservative discourse that resonates with the whole nation. This is why traditional right-wing parties are more resistant to populism than left-wing parties, as the core demands of the movement are more compatible with their agenda than with that of a left that has long since turned its back on the nation. Before rebelling against the system, it is a conservative, nationalist worldview that unites populist voters, a desire to return to normality in the face of a world, which they no longer recognize.[50]

Some institutional actors have even managed to channel the energy of populism to their advantage. Before Boris Johnson, there was Nicolas Sarkozy in 2007, who managed to attract votes from the National Front in the first round of the presidential election. However, as these two examples have shown, the counter-elite that will break the trend taken by Western nations is not yet in control.

Sarkozy failed to live up to expectations and was accused of betraying the patriotic voters he pried away from Le Pen,[51] and the British Tories, under the leadership of Liz Truss and Rishi Sunak, have blown up their electoral base. The announcement of significant tax cuts for the wealthiest, a sharp rise in immigration despite promises to the contrary, and the appointment of former anti-Brexit Prime Minister David Cameron as a minister sent negative signals to the new Conservative coalition. This breach of trust enabled Reform UK, led by Nigel Farage, to attract more than 4 million votes in 2024, at the expense of the Conservatives, who suffered the worst defeat in their history.

If the promised revolution is slow to materialize, it is largely because the political elites remain distant from the people they aspire to represent, both materially and ideologically. In the United Kingdom, for example, 90 percent of MPs are university graduates, compared with only 25 percent of the population. This divide has political consequences: "Conservative MPs are more closely aligned with the average Labour voter than with their own voters."[52] In France, following the 2024 legislative elections, 68 percent of members of the National Assembly were executives or held a higher intellectual profession, whereas this is only the case for 11 percent of French people.[53] Added to this sociological factor is the fact that the traditional right, despite its repeated calls for renewal, seems incapable of presenting a coherent doctrine adapted to the populist moment, in order to institutionalize it and fulfill the desire for reform that it carries within it. Yet this is a goal that it is best placed to pursue, as it has the structure that populists still lack. It embodies a counter-elite rather than a counter-culture.

The Nietzschean Peril

Another dilemma faces conservatives today: If the excesses of the contemporary left are indeed the product of "Christian virtues gone mad," how can they be resisted while preserving Western heritage? For some opponents of wokeism, the thinking of Friedrich Nietzsche may seem appealing. By absolving the strong of any duty toward the weak, it acts as the exact opposite of the ideology of human rights and the ethics of authenticity. However, Nietzsche's philosophy retains what is corrosive to the social fabric, namely a vision of the world as a zero-sum game and an aversion to morality, democracy, and anything that transcends the individual. We often forget that the "philosopher with a hammer" is one of the "masters of suspicion" who most inspired Michel Foucault and the great countercultural thinkers, because his philosophy completely subverts the humanist matrix of our civilization.[54]

Fundamentally, Nietzsche tells us, Judeo-Christian civilization is guilty of being built on the denial of a natural hierarchy, "the aristocratic equation of values"[55] according to which the strong have the right, if not the duty, to dominate the weak. However, Christianity has given birth to a "slave morality," a doctrine that favors "the herd animal" at the expense of the individual with an exceptional destiny: "The mediocre prevail and dictate their own criteria of value."[56] The founding creed of the West was thus born of "the resentment of the masses" and then spread over the centuries through "the poison of the doctrine of 'equal rights for all.'"[57] This means that transcendent morality does not exist, that there is no nobility in the strong protecting the weak. On the contrary, they would harm their own interests and be cruelly manipulated: "morality is manipulative, a way of one person or group exerting power over another, covering this manipulation with the veneer of transcendent authority."[58] This reasoning is the doppelgänger of Marx's dichotomous thinking, which to this day infuses wokeism and pushes for a dead-end confrontation. There is no common good possible, because those who accept a social order that is "detrimental" to their impulses "lose their instincts" and become strangers to themselves.[59]

In the Nietzschean point of view, the tragedy of our time is that, despite the death of God in our secularized societies, we continue to adhere to the Christian ethic of compassion and concern for the weakest among us. The solution to Western decadence would therefore lie in the emancipation of morality: "The reaffirmation of all that is natural and healthy depends on the eradication of these unnatural sources of resentment and degeneration."[60] Once freed from the moral codes that reduce them to the level of the masses, a small elite of strong individuals could finally "rise to the challenge of self-creation, of being whoever they choose to be," without any "obligation to conform to the standards or criteria of anybody else."[61] The Übermensch extolled by Nietzsche is therefore the insular man, the one who transgresses prohibitions to be his own master and who creates himself, *ex nihilo*. It is therefore not surprising that he was embraced by the libertarian left in the 1960s. They saw him as "a thinker of liberation or emancipation, but also of free creation, the quest for an intense life, joyful affirmation, and self-fulfillment. And also a Nietzsche of transgression, insubordination, and subversion."[62] With his contempt for established morality, the weak, and conformists, he is certainly a theorist of the revolt of the elites, not of resistance to it. Hating what the West has become, he does not want to save it, but to hasten its downfall. It would be wrong to believe that Nietzscheanism could be an antidote to wokeism, since it operates according to the same subversive matrix.

Yet, particularly in the United States, Nietzsche's thinking is making a comeback on the fringes of intellectual life and on social media. In a resentful reaction to the woke phenomenon, influencers such as Andrew Tate loudly assert the "right to domination" of so-called dominant groups over those whom the left presents as dominated. There is certainly something predictable about this, insofar as resentment attracts resentment. Nevertheless, this sterile reaction can in no way defend a civilization in which it does not itself believe. Leading Catholic conservative intellectuals such as Sohrab Ahmari and Matthew Schmitz are among the most uncompromising critics of this Nietzschean right, which is incompatible with the populist agenda and the West's Christian ethics. First of all, the vast majority of those who engage in this praise of natural hierarchies do not come from the middle and working classes, and do not speak on their behalf. They are often disillusioned members of the "cognitive class," who find it insufficiently combative, much like the eugenicists of the late nineteenth century.[63] For obvious reasons, this ideology flourishes only among elites or those who consider themselves to be such.

This gives rise to the great paradox of right-wing Nietzscheanism in the era of the *Revolt of the Elites*: "Because the Nietzschean right venerates power and abhors weakness, it is ineluctably drawn to the forces it purports to oppose."[64] With the left dominating civil society, universities, government, and the media, how could the self-proclaimed defenders of the "strong" identify with a right wing that has become the party of the middle and working classes, of the rural regions against the big cities? One example is Richard Spencer, an American white supremacist and one of the main organizers of the controversial Charlottesville demonstration in 2017. In recent years, he has shifted to the left, culminating in his public support for Kamala Harris in 2024. Why such a drastic change? "Conservatives have never seen a lost cause they didn't love . . . They have a libido for anything that is hopeless, flawed beyond repair, and clearly a dead-end."[65] In other words, anyone who worships power above all else in our era cannot truly be a conservative. Nietzscheanism today appears to be just one countercultural stance among many, one that follows the corrosive spirit of the times rather than rebelling against it.

The German philosopher, "resolutely anti-humanist" and "a determined enemy of the democratic idea," is neither conservative nor populist. On the contrary, when he is taken up by the right, it is to serve as a scathing critique of the conservative right of Judeo-Christian culture.[66] Faced with thinkers attached to civilization and morality, who would like to reverse their decline, Nietzscheans respond that, on the contrary, it must be accelerated in order to directly attack the sources of Western tradition. Jean-François Lyotard, a French thinker of postmodernity, describes what he sees as a Nietzschean policy:

> Here is a political line: harden, aggravate, accelerate decadence. Embody active nihilism, do not remain at the simple observation, depressive or admiring, of the destruction of values: put your hand to the destruction, go ever further in disbelief, fight against the restoration of values. Let us march quickly and far in this direction, let us be enterprising in decadence, let us accept, for example, to destroy belief in truth in all its forms.[67]

For anyone who loves the West and wishes to preserve the culture and institutions that provide ordinary people with the essential benchmarks of a stable society, Nietzscheanism cannot be an option, like other harmful temptations that risk betraying the grievances at the root of populism. Former Canadian Prime Minister Stephen Harper sums up the task of the right today: "Populism will be with us in one form or another for some time to come. That is to say, it will be with us as long as working men, women, and families continue to face current economic and social pressures, and conventional political parties do not adapt. And if they do not, troubling elements of the populist agenda could prove more potent in the hands of more focused political operators."[68] The current situation therefore calls for a conservatism focused on the condition of ordinary people and on preserving the norms and culture that support their way of life. In the words of Chantal Delsol, it is that of gardeners, "people who love the world" and who are interested in cultivating it rather than remaking it anew.[69]

CHAPTER 7

Common Good Conservatism

CONSERVATISM IN THE twenty-first century must, above all, be grounded on a sound diagnosis: the revolt of the elites and the breakdown of the norms and institutions that give meaning to the lives of the national middle classes. Some intellectuals who were once on the right, who loyally fought totalitarianism in the twentieth century, seem furiously incapable of breaking out of this outdated prism and see the conservative revival as the "twilight of democracy,"[1] as if negative freedom were the only value worth preserving in our era. The task before us today, on the contrary, is to rebuild social bonds, which necessarily implies appreciating the relevance of certain prohibitions necessary for virtue. While individualism in the legal sense remains a necessity in democracy, it can no longer be the be-all and end-all of politics. This is the meaning of a doctrine known as "post-liberal," which instead turns its gaze toward the common good as an ideal to be achieved, and put back in the center of civilization.

A Policy for the Commons

To make the transition from populism as a protest movement to a form of conservatism that incorporates populism's aims, the concept of the common good is central. This term, sometimes associated with the left at a time when the right was fighting the "revolt of the masses," nevertheless has a deeply conservative meaning today, because it ties in with established norms, the place of common people within the political order, and the cultural survival of Western nations. These are all demands brought about by the populist wave. The "common" has two complementary meanings, just like norms: it is both what is shared by a population and what is ordinary, in the sense of average.[2] The common good is therefore the good of the commons, "the good life that is not 'extraordinary,' but common, generalizable, widely achievable by most humans in a generally decent society."[3] It also implies a rehabilitation of common sense in politics—that practical knowledge that is forged over generations with the traditions of a people and which is the prerogative of everyone, not just a caste of experts.

Respecting common sense therefore means accepting that the role of the state is not to force "progress" on an imperfect people afflicted with multiple "phobias," but rather to be the institutional embodiment of its common good, the structure that is responsible for it and must defend it when it is threatened by antisocial tendencies. This is not a return to the past, but a "return to the center." It also involves a form of rootedness in the nation and in the promise of posterity that it holds for the humble and all those who do not expect their names to appear in the history books. In a secular age, the nation is a common good that ensures everyone their share of eternity, in the certainty that this particular human group that they have helped to build will outlive them and that future generations will continue on the same path.[4] In short, the common good represents the concern for the material as well as cultural prosperity of the majority middle classes who carry the nation.

If we can truly speak of a conservatism of the common good, it is because, as Edmund Burke already sensed, the commons "are the most instinctively conservative element in a social and political order. They seek stability, predictability, and order within the context of a system that is broadly fair."[5] Bringing them back to the forefront implies an ideological realignment within the right, which championed negative freedom in the Reagan and Thatcher era and embraced a vision of change that conserved very little: "The cult of movement for movement's sake, the exaltation of rushing headlong into what is commonly called 'modernization,' the categorical imperative to 'move with the times.'"[6] On the contrary, the conservatism needed today detaches itself from the idea of progress, to which it is rather indifferent, in order to embrace the desire for stability that is shared by the vast majority of citizens. Rather than seeking to free individuals from their roots, it is above all a question of "shoring up the conditions that make freedom possible. These conditions are the institutions of social life: families, communities, nations, and the virtues that sustain them."[7] Public authority, as guardian of the common good, must therefore ensure the social, economic, and cultural conditions for a good life, ordered according to each nation's common good. It does not require transforming the people into anything other than what it already is.

Common good conservatism therefore emphasizes tradition and transmission, and implies renouncing "the ingratitude of strong minds, who forget where the freedom they have conquered comes from." This is not a doctrine imposed by an eccentric minority, but rather by those who have "the humility to recognize themselves as heirs to this treasure that precedes us, accumulated for us over millennia by the work of men walking toward their own humanity."[8] At the heart of this legacy is what George Orwell called common decency,[9] which could be described as a set of unwritten rules that encourage people to care for their neighbors, both in the public and private spheres. This is a widely shared moral concern, akin to common sense, which is shocked by blatant injustices and the antisocial behavior of "selfish rebels" who break the social contract or commit immoral acts, particularly in the economic sphere, whether legal or not. Consider tax evasion or blatantly immoral practices such as those of American entrepreneur Martin Shkreli, who legally bought drug patents and increased their prices tenfold, forcing many sick people into poverty.[10] Common decency, in a way, is an auxiliary to the ethics of duty, reminding us that just because an action can be committed without legal consequences does not mean it is right. Above all, it draws attention to the fact that interactions on a human scale tend toward equality and consideration for others, and that a fairer world must come from below rather than being imposed from above, at a level too far removed from the way common people live.

In its economic doctrine, common good conservatism therefore distances itself from a certain "elitist right," whose agenda tends to be that of big business against ordinary people, with massively unpopular proposals such as making it easier to fire employees or increasing working hours.[11] This social concern, which is truly conservative, is not the Marxists' appetite for revolution, nor, more broadly, that of the left for victims. Rather, it stems from the conservative preference for authority and order over subversion,[12] following the example of the social doctrine of Pope Leo XIII, which sought to offer workers a decent wage and the right to unionize so that social harmony would triumph over revolutionary zeal.[13] This is also the sentiment of the left wing of Gaullism in France, which favored employee participation in companies in the name of a certain vision of justice, but also of social order. Conversely, when inequalities increase significantly in a given nation, instability and violence ensue. The social-democratic bargain is proof that this theory works, as the working classes were so satisfied with it that they abandoned the revolutionary ideal. The conflictual logic inherent in left-wing thought is not widely shared among the population, whose concern for equality stems from a desire for order. The nation is also a powerful factor in equality, as a shared culture breeds solidarity among its members. Conversely, there is a tension between pluralism and solidarity, which David Goodhart calls the "progressive dilemma":

> This is America versus Sweden. You can have a Swedish welfare state provided you are a homogeneous society with intensely shared values. In the US you have a very diverse, individualistic society where people feel fewer obligations to fellow citizens. Progressives want diversity but they thereby undermine part of the moral consensus on which a large welfare state rests.[14]

Contrary to what Marxists claim, adherence to the nation is therefore not a form of alienation for the poor, but rather comes from a "powerful material motivation."[15] They are the first to benefit from the redistribution of wealth made possible by national solidarity, when the wealthiest identify with their plight and therefore agree to pay a larger portion of their income in taxes. Without a common identification with the nation, this solidarity evaporates.

Virtue and Freedom

To build the common good, we must also set aside a certain conception of individual rights that serves "selfish rebels" in opposition to the fundamental institutions of society. The good of the family, the community, and the nation reinforces the good of the individual, and we must therefore think about individual rights accordingly.

Rather than constituting "trumps" that allow individuals to escape collective obligations, according to Ronald Dworkin's thinking, freedoms are part of a decent society, since the common good can only be achieved by allowing everyone a sphere of privacy and freedom. Freedom, properly understood, unlike negative freedom, does not aim to escape society, but rather the good of the whole, and is framed by a vision of what is acceptable in a just order.[16] For conservatives, society is not a contract from which one can opt out as he wishes, but rather the essential framework that precedes freedoms and without which they could not exist. The same applies to moral law.

The freedom to do good is not equivalent to the freedom to do evil, and "the one thing that counts" is not "whether the invention is made in the name of freedom,"[17] as Sartrean existentialism claims. Aristotle believed that the law's role was to create good habits,[18] in order to "prescribe and prohibit certain types of action absolutely and such actions are among those which a virtuous man would do or refrain from doing."[19] Adrian Vermeule, professor of law at Harvard and theorist of common good constitutionalism, speaks of "a candid willingness to 'legislate morality.'"[20] This implies, first of all, moving away from the damaging "harm reduction" approach favored by liberals, which essentially consists of legalizing traditionally prohibited vices on the grounds that it is better to see them in the open, or even institutionalize them, than to allow them to occur illegally. This premise is false, first because legalizing a practice leads to its proliferation among a mass of people who would have refrained from it if it were prohibited by law, particularly in the case of illicit substance use. Once an antisocial practice is sanctioned by law, it loses its taboo status in the eyes of the majority, a symptom of an era in which morality is unfortunately becoming less and less distinct from legality:

> Every conflict is solved according to the letter of the law and this is considered to be the ultimate solution. If one is right

> from a legal point of view, nothing more is required, nobody may mention that one could still not be entirely right, and urge self-restraint or a renunciation of these rights, call for sacrifice and selfless risk: This would simply sound absurd. Voluntary self-restraint is almost unheard of: Everybody strives toward further expansion to the extreme limit of the legal frames.[21]

While this observation is certainly distressing, it reminds us of the essential role of legal prohibitions, which sometimes seem to be the only barrier capable of stopping the self-expansion lamented by Solzhenitsyn. It should also be noted that the law, even if it is not rigorously enforced, acts as a norm that citizens can then apply among themselves. It can strengthen the moral fabric at the local level. In 1978, San Francisco required all its citizens, under penalty of a fine, to pick up their dogs' feces, which was of course unenforceable by the police, but which motivated citizens to do so themselves and to reprimand those who refused to comply.[22] The state therefore has a role to play as an enforcer of norms. A moral awakening within the state can help change this dynamic and stimulate virtue in society.

Moreover, there is always a way of life that is implicitly valued by public policies, whether in the receipt of social transfers, taxation, or government communications. The Council of Europe's "Freedom in the Hijab" advertising campaign, which promoted the Islamic veil using public funds, is a telling counterexample.[23] Too often, public authorities imagine themselves in the role of social engineers and display a spectacular disconnect from the values shared by the people, which they expect to see respected at the state level. This does nothing to improve the already stifling cynicism toward politics, which feeds on these instances where leaders send a clear signal to the majority of citizens that they are not working for them. A state serving the common good would, on the contrary, make the life of the common people the "default" way of life on which it bases its policies.

We can already anticipate the liberal objection: Should we really give so much power to the state and risk it falling into the wrong hands? No constitution or doctrine can guarantee that the law will only be used for good purposes, or that leaders will always act in the public interest, even if we increase the number of checks and balances. Above all, the elitist drift of recent decades should remind us that the power taken away from elected government is never really given back to citizens. Rather, it is monopolized by institutions belonging to representatives of the cognitive class, such as courts and state agencies. Their leaders, unlike members of Parliament or Congress, are not elected by the people, who have no say in their conduct. Electoral democracy makes citizens the ultimate counterweight to power, and it cannot exist without maximal freedom of expression. This freedom, which undoubtedly belongs more to the ancients than to the moderns according to Benjamin Constant's typology, is the indispensable condition for democracy, because it is what allows for deliberation on common rules. Is it any surprise that today's so-called progressive defenders of rights and freedoms are so quick to censor it in the name of the discomfort of some? Freedom of expression therefore is the point of contact between the individual and the collective, demonstrating that there is no opposition between the individual and democracy as long as the individual can take part in deliberation.

Similarly, democracy cannot survive without national culture. Too many social contract theorists have taken culture for granted, as if random individuals spontaneously gathered with people who had nothing in common with them to create a society *ex nihilo*. On the contrary, in order to deliberate on the common good, there must already be a bond between them, so that they see their interest in the decisions of the whole.[24] Without roots and belonging, freedom and virtue become impossible and give way to a politics of recognition that boils down to a clash of subjectivities, a contemporary form of the "war of all against all" that modern political thought sought above all to avoid.

Balancing Community and Nation

While the value of rootedness is unanimously accepted in conservative circles, the scale on which it should be anchored is sometimes debated, as in the eternal French quarrel between the Girondins and the Jacobins. The Girondins are primarily concerned with "the gradual disappearance of local cultures and deep-rooted ways of life," while the Jacobins are more alarmed today by "the destabilization of large cultural blocs and the decline of the nation-state."[25] While French republicans are ostensibly defenders of the nation above all else, there is nevertheless a widely shared sentiment, especially lively in the Anglosphere, which values locality and communities on a human scale. Patrick Deneen, for example, expresses a certain skepticism about the primacy of the nation insofar as it "was originally a key aspect of the liberal political project,"[26] and that the nation-state has often had a tendency toward uniformity, at the expense of local communities and families. Thinkers such as Alasdair MacIntyre even withdraw their trust in the state and the nation, judging them to be so corrupted by liberal dissolution that they threaten families and communities attempting to live truly moral lives.[27] However, drawing a firm line between the family or local community and the nation would remove conservatism from the political arena and confine it to the private sphere, akin to a form of counterculture or sectarianism, which would simply make it impossible to establish norms that order society as a whole. Under the guise of illiberalism, this hyperlocalist temptation accepts the libertarian premise that the common good cannot be found on the scale of an entire society, but is rather confined to small, select communities. To act in the common interest, there must be a commonality, and this is what the nation-state allows.

Above all, since conservatism aims to preserve tradition, it is not a universal ideology, unlike Marxism or liberalism, which are conceived as doctrines that can be applied everywhere, at all times, in the same way. On the contrary, traditions vary from one place to another, and a proper conservatism has no choice but to preserve them in their uniqueness.[28] Almost all nations are also based on a cultural core and organic ties on a human scale, which the nation-state has managed to preserve and must continue to cherish for the good of the common people, who value these affiliations. If it were to detach itself from these loyalties or wage a crusade against them, it would cease to fulfill its role and sink into tyranny. The political nation is not just an abstraction; is it an intermediary between inherited tradition and universal citizenship. The same applies to French-style *laïcité* (secularism), which is eternally misunderstood in the Anglosphere: its critics describe it as too abstract and liberal, if they are conservative, or too restrictive and associated with a normative vision, if they are liberal. Let us recall "the intrinsic link between *laïcité* and the civilizational substratum from which it originated"; this philosophy does not come from nowhere, but from a fundamentally Christian "civilizational background."[29] It is therefore not an abstract value, but rather a legacy resulting from a particular history. This specifically "identity-based" aspect of *laïcité*, which was born of no religious tradition other than Christianity, explains why the mainstream left is more skeptical than ever about it, since it conflicts with minority demands. It sees it as particularism disguised as universalism, like integration to the nation.

More fundamentally, the common good cannot be conceived in the absence of a common culture. For Aristotle, the city depended on civic friendship, and it goes without saying that people who have nothing in common also have no friendship between them.[30] To coexist within a political community united around a vision of the good, it is necessary to share a culture and values. Robert Putnam's work has shown that excessive ethnocultural pluralism, without shared identification with the same group, leads to a decline in the level of trust between citizens, including within the same community.[31] A historical perspective also shows that the volume of immigration is inversely proportional to social cohesion in the United States in the twentieth century:[32] a significant reduction from the 1920s onward allowed for the integration of those who were already present and the construction of a stronger national sentiment until the mid-century upheaval, coinciding with the growth in immigration flows after 1965. The social democratic bargain was made possible precisely because nations, while not completely homogeneous, had a stronger sense of unity than today, partly because the norms of the majority were valued, contrary to an imperative of authenticity that discourages integration through the institutional promotion of diversity.

In this sense, significantly reducing the amount of immigration accepted by the West has become an absolute necessity in order to maintain a certain level of social cohesion. David Goodhart rightly points out that nations' capacity for integration is not unlimited: when minority populations exceed 30 percent in a neighborhood, school, or any other institution, they develop a self-sufficiency that allows them to exist outside local norms.[33] Without meaningful integration, the common good becomes impossible, as is already the case in some Canadian cities, where politics boils down to communitarian and diasporic demands, to the point where commentators like Tasha Kheiriddin describe the country as "a balkanized grievance factory."[34] The adoption of the Palestinian cause by the political left throughout the West, as a subtle way of mobilizing a Muslim electorate on a sectarian basis, is another striking example, notably with the election of four "pro-Gaza independent MPs" in the last British elections. The lack of cohesion even harms minorities, according to Putnam, who notes that when integration is successful, national majorities are more likely to care about the fate of their immigrant fellow citizens and to want to fight against the discrimination they may suffer.[35] Conversely, sectarianism and the ethic of authenticity provoke the rejection of minority demands because they are based on a desire for differentiation that runs counter to the universality of citizenship.

In line with their defense of the common good, conservatives must impose cultural conditions on citizenship and immigration. Insofar as the state is the institutional incarnation of a particular nation, it is under no obligation to accept as members those who have no intention of joining it. This is already the principle of French-style assimilation, which Dominique Schnapper describes as the acceptance of the other as similar and not as different,[36] which has lost its vigor as the new mainstream is centered on authenticity and non-integration. Vincent Coussedière calls integration an "inclusive exclusion"[37] toward foreigners, in the sense that, for it to have value and be fully inclusive, it necessarily implies the exclusion of practices, customs, or ways of life that are not compatible with the nation that is to be preserved. The "frank desire to 'legislate on morality'" must therefore be accompanied by an equivalent desire to legislate on culture, in order to make clear which model is valued by the community. The common good cannot exist outside the national framework, which is why common good conservatism must also be a national conservatism.

Reconciling the People and the Elite

Since at least 2010, the West has been going through an unresolved populist period, which has degenerated into an escalation of polarization detrimental to society:

> We find ourselves in a worrying vicious circle: the people's abysmal mistrust of their leaders is propelling insurgents onto the political scene. The elites respond by attacking these new leaders and their voters, instead of formulating a response to the latter's anxieties—which only increases mistrust. As philosopher Pierre Manent notes, we are caught between the "contempt" of the former and the "anger" of the latter.[38]

This inability to communicate reminds us that those who govern and those who are governed are complementary bodies that need each other. Without leaders with the technical knowledge and vision to govern the country, the people always run the risk of sinking into the leveling that Tocqueville feared in the democratic experiment. This is the nihilistic temptation mentioned earlier, a "contrarian" politics without ideological content, fueled exclusively by the rejection of the leaders in power. Conversely, when they are detached from the people, those in power believe themselves to be all-powerful and govern solely in their own interests, to the detriment of the common good. What Aristotle calls "the mixed constitution" allows the two bodies to control each other, for the good of the whole, so that neither wishes to live under another regime where it could crush the other.[39] This, in fact, was the original inspiration behind representative democracy: the election of representatives allows citizens to have the final say on who governs them, but it also institutionalizes an elite separate from the governed, in the form of elected officials.[40]

If we consider that a growing schism between the governed and the governing is at the heart of the current disorder, then the solution to the populist wave cannot be found in a form of direct democracy or a rejection of representative democracy. Such an exercise, except perhaps in Switzerland, always ends up being hijacked by activists and professional pressure groups, who in no way represent the will of the majority, mirroring the capture of civil society by the cognitive class mentioned before. The beauty of representative democracy is precisely that the little commitment it requires from the people gives a voice to the silent majority and serves as a safeguard against active minorities, who are highly mobilized but few in number. However, representatives must still be up to the task.

If the West wants to emerge from this populist moment, its elites must be reminded of their responsibility to preserve the cultural traditions and common good for which they are responsible. Patrick Deneen rightly wants them to "understand that their main role and purpose in the social order is to secure the foundational goods that make possible human flourishing for ordinary people."[41] Régis Debray sums up the same idea in another way: "France is only great when there is an alliance between the sovereign and the plebeian . . . When the two divorce, there is danger. The plebs become the populace . . . and the sovereign becomes autocratic."[42] This system, in which the rulers and the ruled coexist and collaborate, is in reality nothing other than representative democracy as it should function, and as it functioned before a homogeneous and secluded elite seized it. Joseph Schumpeter rightly argued that representative democracy is in fact a competition between elites and that the real power of citizens consists above all in "throwing the rascals out" when they govern badly.[43] If there is to be reconciliation between the people and the elite, it will come through common good conservatism, and above all through a return to the essence of representative democracy, where elites must think about their policies for the commons, not for an "enlightened" minority.

After more than a decade of bitter clashes over identity politics, could we soon see a certain "consensus" emerge among the political parties aspiring to power, in the form of an implicit admission of failure by the progressive elites, who would rally to conservative positions out of pragmatism? The failure of the policy of containment is now clear: wherever left-wing parties have taken up the cause of identity or societal progressivism to confront the right, they have lost the favor of the middle and working classes. What's more, those who pursue a libertarian agenda are quickly caught up by reality: The decriminalization of drugs and the weakening of sovereign power jeopardize citizens' safety, mass immigration creates a crises in housing and public services, and gender ideology leads minors to make drastic choices that they later regret. Faced with the failure of the progressive project of a liquid society, without constraints or identity, the political left may well be forced, as in the 1990s, to practice "triangulation"[44] like Bill Clinton or Tony Blair, and essentially concede victory to the right on morals and identity in order to fall back on public services and the economy.

The tectonic plates are already beginning to shift. After ten years of trumpeting the virtues of multiculturalism and open borders, Canadian Prime Minister Justin Trudeau announced in 2024 a substantial reduction in immigration, continued by his Liberal successor, Mark Carney.[45] Upon coming to power, British Labour leader Keir Starmer made permanent the Conservatives' temporary ban on "puberty blockers" for transgender minors.[46] California's Democratic governor and White House hopeful Gavin Newsom has set aside his anti-police and anti-prison positions to mobilize law enforcement against drug trafficking and violent crime.[47] The tide is turning in the West. This growing consensus for more order, identity, and security proves that the foundations of communal life cannot be dissolved without consequences. To avoid the "war of all against all" feared by Hobbes, the solution has hardly changed in four centuries: the sublimation of impulses and subjectivities by means of moral and written laws that ensure the good of the whole. In other words, civilization.

Conclusion

AFTER HALF A CENTURY of deconstruction, Western civilization is no longer the same. This process of anti-civilization has progressed in many ways, leading to an unfortunate outcome: the erosion of common goods such as social capital, trust, security, and even culture. Without this collective heritage, how can we live together? And, above all, how can we live a fulfilling life? In the name of freedom and diversity, we collectively bet that human flourishing would remain possible outside our local, cultural, and social roots. The future has proven the opposite: Generation Z, the author's own generation, is probably the most desocialized in recent history, due to the deliberate refusal of its elders to pass on tradition and culture. The sad situation of young people born between 1995 and 2012, who are now beginning to make their voices heard in the public sphere, shows that their predecessors got it all wrong: human beings do not create themselves from a blank slate, they cannot be happy by themselves, and they cannot flourish outside their nurturing roots. The Western world is ripe for the return of a culture of normality, which will finally put ordinary people back at the heart of democracy.

The Atomized Generation

Generation Z is reaping the fruits sown by the baby boomers, the "sixties generation,"[1] who, in their libertarian fervor, broke the chain of transmission without realizing that the cultural and moral heritage they had received was precisely the condition of their freedom. As generations succeed one another, the traces of this precious heritage fade, and young people are orphaned of the civilizational transmission they desperately need. The idea that culture, established customs, and civilization are burdens for human beings ultimately proves to be the greatest of "luxury beliefs." Because we took these treasures for granted and neglected to maintain them, we sorely miss them today. The breakdown of value systems and social relationships has left behind a field of ruins. Several studies conducted among young Americans, at the forefront of Western trends, point to a worrying impoverishment of social ties. They have fewer close friends[2] and see their friends less often than before.[3] Love is also in decline: young people have less sex than their elders did at the same age, and even young people in relationships are sleeping together less and less.[4] It seems that "social distancing," a term coined during the pandemic, has become an established reality.

A product of technological innovations in recent years, the desocialized generation is also hyperconnected, to the detriment of genuine human bonds. The advent of social media, online commerce, and texting has enabled the pursuit of a "mediated" existence, lived through a technological intermediary rather than directly. Sixty-five percent of Gen Zers avoid phone calls, which make them uncomfortable, preferring the extra distance offered by texting.[5] Many apps have turned this growing social unease into their business model, which is to "satisfy consumers ever more quickly by sparing them the necessity of collective interactions."[6] Uber Eats not only spares us cooking, but also having to leave the house to go to the grocery store or even to buy takeout. Tinder, Bumble, Hinge, and similar apps offer to dispense with the mystery of seduction in favor of *à la carte* relationships in a controlled market that has become the most important meeting place for young people.[7] The Québécois app Partage Club is a caricatured embodiment of this trend, offering a paid online platform for . . . borrowing items from your neighbors, which didn't require an intermediary just a few years ago.[8] We are facing "extreme fragmentation of the collective space [which] obviously does not allow society to survive, as it loses the informal rules that structure social bonds."[9] Unsurprisingly, a desocialized civilization is also one that has fewer and fewer children, and where people are becoming parents later and later, now after thirty years old in most of the Western world.[10]

Has the "open society" made us happier? On the contrary, Generation Z is swept away by a nihilistic temptation, more inclined to believe that life has no meaning, to doubt themselves, and to take a pessimistic view of the future.[11] It would seem that individualism has created a need for identity, belonging, and reference points that has not been fulfilled by the void that has been offered to them. The impoverishment of general culture, a worthy offspring of a presentism that dismisses the great works of the Western canon, goes hand in hand with a closing of the mind and horizons,[12] which makes us incapable of communing with what came before us: "Our ignorance renders statues mute, images indecipherable, texts incomprehensible; the signs we have inherited lose their meaning."[13] This "precariousness of all spheres of existence"[14] logically translates into a "demand for protection, measure, and limits"[15] to serve as a guide in an unknown and strange world to which they have been deliberately denied the keys. Left to fend for themselves in a labyrinth without a map to guide them, young people have every right to hold this new world accountable for abandoning them.

More and more observers are realizing that the younger generations reject the progressive project as much, if not more, than their elders and are among the most enthusiastic supporters of the populist shift to the right. In the 2024 US election, no less than 56 percent of men and 40 percent of women under the age of thirty cast a Republican ballot,[16] whereas in 2008, 60 percent of young people had voted for Barack Obama.[17] The first voters to rally behind Donald Trump in 2015 were, in fact, Americans who were "civically disengaged" and who experience the most severe social isolation.[18] In France, the National Rally can count on voters who are significantly younger than those of Emmanuel Macron, to the point of challenging the far-left La France Insoumise as the "party of youth."[19] In Canada, the arrival of Pierre Poilievre at the head of the Conservative Party has given rise to the same phenomenon: for the first time in recent history, young Canadians are voting more to the right than their elders.[20] Contrary to all expectations, it seems that more and more young people, disenchanted with the broken promises of deconstruction, agree with Patrick Deneen that liberalism has failed,[21] and wish as Robert Putnam does for an "upswing"[22] in Western civilization.

Rebuilding Civilization on the Ruins of Deconstruction

A revival, on an individual and collective scale, requires above all a break with the concept of the atomized individual in perpetual struggle with the institutions that surround him. The present times call for a truly "post-liberal" reflection, which will dare to ask once again the question that was taboo for the great liberal thinkers of the last century: what should I do with my freedom? How can I lead a good life as a free person? In line with Western tradition, from Aristotle to Christianity, let us think of a humanity and individuality that strengthens society rather than setting itself against it: "We are most fully human when we contribute to the common good and thus earn the esteem of our fellow citizens for the contributions we make. According to this tradition, the fundamental human need is to be needed by those with whom we share a common life."[23] This therefore implies reversing the trend toward individual secession, in order to rebuild community and mutual responsibilities, instead of commodifying solidarity through digital intermediaries. This means that there is no natural right to non-integration, contrary to what the theorists of multiculturalism claim. Those who join a nation and benefit from its social model must, in return, agree to embrace its customs. This also means that the value of elites is measured by their contribution to the common good, not by the amount of prestige or capital they manage to accumulate for themselves. As Rod Dreher explains, "Civilization doesn't exist to make it possible for individuals to do whatever they want to do. To believe that is an anthropological error. A civilization in which no one felt an obligation to the past, to the future, to each other, or to anything higher than self-gratification is one that is dangerously fragile."[24]

In order to learn once again how to live together, because that is what this is all about, we can fortunately still count on the first institution where the common good is lived out, which is also the last holistic institution we still know,[25] the family. Against all odds, it remains the indestructible rock on which human beings can rely, never truly conquered by the spirit of the times, constructivism, or individualism. "The family is a determinism that, by definition, cannot be broken. It is a matter of nature, even more so than culture. And it remains biological in its essence. Like birth, gender differences, old age, and death, it is immutable."[26] It is the ideal place for a culture of normality to be reborn, because it is the school of responsibility and virtue through which we learn that what has real value is what money cannot buy. It is by giving selflessly to our children, parents, siblings, or grandparents that we can truly grasp the meaning of the common good, namely that life has no meaning if it is lived for oneself, in suspicion of what has gone before and what will follow.

According to British philosopher Roger Scruton, conservatism is above all the doctrine of love, for what we share, what defines us, and what we will leave to those who follow us.[27] It is from this love that we must draw to rebuild civilization, a love widely shared among ordinary people who, sheltered from politics, preserve precious treasures of knowledge, decency, and common sense. As long as it exists, civilization will stand firm against the forces that seek to deconstruct it.

Bibliography

Books

ADORNO, Theodor W., *The Authoritarian Personality*, New York, Harper, 1950.

AHMARI, Sohrab, *Tyranny Inc. How Private Power Crushed American Liberty—and What to Do About It*, New York, Forum Books, 2023.

AL-GHARBI, Musa, *We Have Never Been Woke. The Cultural Contradictions of a New Elite*, Princeton, Princeton University Press, 2024.

ANDERSON, Benedict, *Imagined Communities*, Londres, Verso, 1983.

ANNETT, Anthony, *Cathonomics. How Catholic Tradition Can Create a More Just Economy*, Washington, Georgetown University Press, 2021.

APPARU, Benoist (dir.), *Les Douze travaux de l'opposition. Nos projets pour redresser la France*, Paris, Flammarion, 2014.

APPLEBAUM, Anne, *Twilight of Democracy. The Seductive Lure of Authoritarianism*, New York, Doubleday, 2020.

ARENDT, Hannah, *Eichmann in Jerusalem. A Report of the Banality of Evil*, New York, Viking Press, [1963] 1964. Ebook edition.

ARISTOTLE, *The Nicomachean Ethics*, New York, Penguin Books, 2004.

ARISTOTLE, *The Politics*, Oxford, Oxford University Press, 2009.

ARON, Raymond, *Plaidoyer pour l'Europe décadente*, Paris, Robert Laffont, coll. Pluriel, 1977.

ARON, Raymond, *50 ans de réflexion politique. Mémoires*, Paris, Julliard, 1983.

BABEAU, Olivier, *Éloge de l'hypocrisie*, Paris, Cerf, 2018.

BADIE, Bertrand, VIDAL, Dominique (dir.), *Le Retour des populismes: l'État du monde 2019*, Paris, La Découverte, 2018.

BASTIÉ, Eugénie, *Le Porc émissaire. Terreur ou contre-révolution*, Paris, Cerf, 2018.

BASTIÉ, Eugénie, *La Guerre des idées. Enquête au cœur de l'intelligentsia française*, Paris, Robert Laffont, 2021.

BASTIÉ, Eugénie, *La Dictature des ressentis*, Paris, Plon, 2023.

BAUMAN, Zygmunt, *Liquid Life*, London, Polity, 2005.

BAUMAN, Zygmunt, *Strangers at Our Door*, London, Polity, 2016.

BEAUCHEMIN, Jacques, *La Société des identités. Éthique et politique dans le monde contemporain*, Outremont, Athéna, 2004.

BELLAMY, François-Xavier, *Les Déshérités*, Paris, Plon, coll. J'ai lu, 2014.

BELLAMY, François-Xavier, *Espérer*, Paris, Grasset, 2023.

BERLIN, Isaiah, *Liberty*, Oxford, Oxford University Press, [1969] 2008.

BIAGGI, Vladimir (éd.), *Le Nihilisme*, Paris, Flammarion, coll. GF, 2008.

BLOOM, Allan, *The Closing of the American Mind*, New York, Simon & Schuster, 1987.

BOAZ, David, *The Libertarian Mind*, New York, Simon & Schuster, [1997] 2015.

BOCK-CÔTÉ, Mathieu, *Le Multiculturalisme comme religion politique*, Paris, Cerf, 2015.

BOCK-CÔTÉ, Mathieu, *L'Empire du politiquement correct*, Paris, Cerf, 2019.

BOCK-CÔTÉ, Mathieu, *Le Totalitarisme sans le goulag*, Paris, Presses de la Cité, 2023.

BONNARDEL, Yves, LEPELTIER, Thomas, SIGLER, Pierre (dir.), *La Révolution antispéciste*, Paris, Humensis, coll. Alpha, [2018] 2023.

BOUVET, Laurent, *Le Sens du peuple*, Paris, Gallimard, coll. Le Débat, 2012.

BOUVET, Laurent, *La Nouvelle question laïque*, Paris, Flammarion, 2019.

BRADLEY, Gracie May, DE NORONHA, Luke, *Against Borders*, Londres, Verso, 2022.

BRICKER, Darrell, IBBITSON, John, *The Big Shift. The Seismic Change in Canadian Politics, Business, and Culture and What It Means for Our Future*, Toronto, HarperCollins, [2013] 2014.

BROOKS, David, *Bobos in Paradise. The New Upper Class and How They Got There*, New York, Simon & Schuster, [2000] 2004.

BUISSON, Patrick, *La Cause du peuple*, Paris, Perrin, 2016.

BURNHAM, James, *The Managerial Revolution. What Is Happening in the World*, Borough, Lume Books, [1941] 1988.

BUTLER, Judith, *Who's Afraid of Gender?*, London, Allen Lane, 2024.

CALDWELL, Christopher, *The Age of Entitlement. America Since the Sixties*, New York, Simon & Schuster, 2020.

CAMPBELL, Bradley, MANNING, Jason, *The Rise of Victimhood Culture. Microaggressions, Safe Spaces, and the New Culture Wars*, Londres, Palgrave Macmillan, 2018.

CARDINAL, François, MONTIGNY, Éric (dir.), *La Révolution Z. Comment les jeunes transformeront le Québec*, Montréal, La Presse, 2019.

CARGOËT, Antoine, *Recréer le ciel. Genèse et devenir du populisme*, Paris, Cerf, 2022.

CARL, Jeremy, *The Unprotected Class. How Anti-White Racism Is Tearing America Apart*, Washington, Regnery, 2024.

CARNEY, Timothy P., *Family Unfriendly. How Our Culture Made Raising Kids Much Harder Than It Needs to Be*, New York, Harper, 2024.

CHAPOUTOT, Johann, *La Révolution culturelle nazie*, Paris, Gallimard, coll. Tel, 2017.

CHESTERTON, Gilbert Keith, *Heretics*, Albany, SAGE, [1905] 1996.

CHESTERTON, Gilbert Keith, *Orthodoxy*, Dekton, [1908] 2022.

CHOLLET, Mona, *Résister à la culpabilisation*, Paris, La Découverte, coll. Zones, 2024.

ÇOUSSEDIÈRE, Vincent, *Éloge de l'assimilation*, Monaco, Rocher, 2021.

CRAPEZ, Marc, *Je suis un contrariant. Petit précis d'un chercheur à contre-courant*, Paris, Michalon, 2016.

CRAWFORD, Matthew B., *Shop Class as Soulcraft. An Inquiry Into the Value of Work*, New York, Penguin, 2009.

CRAWFORD, Matthew B., *The World Beyond Your Head. On becoming an Individual in an Age of Distraction*, New York, Farrar, Strauss & Giroux, [2014] 2016.

DALRYMPLE, Theodore, *Admirable Evasions*, New York, Encounter, 2015.

DE GUIGNÉ, Anne, *Le Capitalisme woke*, Paris, Presses de la Cité, 2022.

DE LAGASNERIE, Geoffroy, *3. Une invitation au dehors*, Paris, Flammarion, coll. Nouvel Avenir, 2023.

DE TOCQUEVILLE, Alexis, *Democracy in America, vol. 1*, Gutenberg, 1835. https://www.gutenberg.org/ebooks/815.

DEJARDIN, Camille, *John Stuart Mill: libéral utopique*, Paris, Gallimard, coll. Bibliothèque des idées, 2022.

DELSOL, Chantal, *La Haine du monde*, Paris, Cerf, coll. Lexio, [2016] 2019.

DENEEN, Patrick J., *Conserving America? Essays on Present Discontents*, South Bend, St. Augustine's Press, 2016.

DENEEN, Patrick J., *Regime Change. Toward a Postliberal Future*, New York, Sentinel, 2023.

DEVECCHIO, Alexandre, *Les Nouveaux enfants du siècle. Djihadistes, identitaires, réacs. Enquête sur une génération fracturée*, Paris, Cerf, 2016.

DEVECCHIO, Alexandre, *Recomposition. Le nouveau monde populiste*, Paris, Cerf, 2019.

DIANGELO, Robin, *White Fragility. Why It's So Hard for White People to Talk About Racism*, Boston, Beacon Press, 2018.

DONALDSON, Sue, KYMLICKA, Will, *Zoopolis. A Political Theory of Animal Rights*, Oxford, Oxford University Press, 2011.

DOUTHAT, Ross, SALAM, Reihan, *Grand New Party*, New York, Doubleday, 2008.

DOUTHAT, Ross, *The Decadent Society: How We Became the Victims of Our Own Success*, New York, Avid Reader Press, 2020.

DUHAIME, Éric, *La Fin de l'homosexualité et le dernier gay*, Montréal, L'Homme, 2017.

DUROCHER, Sophie, *Où sont les femmes?*, Montréal, Éditions du Journal, 2024.

DREHER, Rod, *The Benedict Option. A Strategy for Christians in a Post-Christian Nation*, New York, Sentinel, 2017.

DWORKIN, Ronald, *Taking Rights Seriously*, Cambridge, Harvard University Press, 1977.

EATWELL, Roger, GOODWIN, Matthew, *National Populism. The Revolt Against Liberal Democracy*, Londres, Pelican, 2018.

EDDÉ, Maroun, *La Mémoire coupable*, Paris, Bouquins, 2022.

ELIAS, Norbert, *The Civilizing Process*, Oxford, Wiley-Blackwell, [1939] 2000.

ELIAS, Norbert, *The Society of Individuals*, New York, Continuum, [1987] 2001.

FAVELL, Adrian, *The Integration Nation. Immigration and Colonial Power in Liberal Democracies*, Cambridge, Polity, 2022.

FERRY, Luc, RENAUT, Alain, *La Pensée 68*, Paris, Flammarion, coll. Folio, [1985] 1988.

FERRY, Luc, *La Frénésie du bonheur. Du bonheur différé au bonheur immédiat*, Paris, Observatoire, 2023.

FITOUSSI, Samuel, *Woke Fiction*, Paris, Cherche-Midi, 2023.

FLORIDA, Richard, *The Rise of the Creative Class*, New York, Basic Books, [2002] 2012.

FOUCAULT, Michel, *Discipline and Punish*, New York, Vintage, [1975] 1995.

FOURQUET, Jérôme, *Le Nouveau clivage*, Paris, Cerf, coll. Lexio, [2018] 2020.

FOURQUET, Jérôme, *L'Archipel français. Naissance d'une nation multiple et divisée*, Paris, Seuil, coll. Points, [2019] 2020.

FREUD, Sigmund, *The Standard Edition of the Complete Psychological Works of Sigmund Freud, Volume XXI (1927-1931): The Future of an Illusion, Civilization and its Discontents, and Other Works*, London, Hogarth, 1961.

GARCIA, Manon, *La Conversation des sexes. Philosophie du consentement*, Paris, Climats, 2021.

GAUCHET, Marcel, *Le Désenchantement du monde*, Paris, Gallimard, coll. Folio, 1985.

GIESBERT, Franz-Olivier, *Tragédie française*, Paris, Gallimard, 2023.

GIRARD, René, *I See Satan Fall Like Lightning*, Maryknoll, Orbis, [1999] 2001.

GIRAUD, Amaury, *Penser le conservatisme à gauche*, Bordeaux, Le Bord de l'eau, 2024.

GOBIN, Julien, *L'individu, fin de parcours? Le piège de l'intelligence artificielle*, Paris, Gallimard, coll. Le Débat, 2024.

GOODHART, David, *The British Dream*, London, Atlantic Books, 2014.

GOODHART, David, *The Road to Somewhere*, London, Hurst, 2017.

GOODHART, David, *Head, Hand, Heart. Why Intelligence Is Over-Rewarded, Manual Workers Matter, and Caregivers Deserve More Respect*, New York, Free Press, 2020.

GOODWIN, Matthew, *Voice, Values and Virtue. The New British Politics*, Londres, Penguin, 2023.

GOTTFRIED, Paul, *Antifascism: The Course of a Crusade*, DeKalb, Northern Illinois University Press, 2021, édition Kindle.

GRIFFIN, Roger, *Fascism*, Cambridge, Polity, 2018.

GUILLUY, Christophe, *La France périphérique. Comment on a sacrifié les classes populaires*, Paris, Flammarion, coll. Champs, [2014] 2015.

GUILLUY, Christophe, *Le Crépuscule de la France d'en-haut*, Paris, Flammarion, coll. Champs, [2016] 2017.

GUILLUY, Christophe, *No Society. La fin de la classe moyenne occidentale*, Paris, Flammarion, coll. Champs, [2018] 2019.

GUILLUY, Christophe, *Le Temps des gens ordinaires*, Paris, Flammarion, 2020.

GUILLUY, Christophe, *Les Dépossédés*, Paris, Flammarion, 2022.

HABIB, Claude, *Le Privé n'est pas politique*, Paris, Gallimard, coll. Le Débat, 2024.

HAIDT, Jonathan, *The Righteous Mind. Why Good People Are Divided by Politics and Religion*, New York, Vintage, [2012] 2013.

HALPERIN, Mark, HARRIS, John F., *The Way to Win. Taking the White House in 2008*, New York, Random House, 2006.

HANANIA, Richard, *The Origins of Woke. Civil Rights Law, Corporate America and the Triumph of Identity Politics*, New York, Broadside, 2023.

HARPER, Stephen, *Right Here, Right Now. Politics and Leadership in the Age of Disruption*, Toronto, Signal, 2018.

HARRINGTON, Mary, *Feminism Against Progress*, Washington, Regnery, 2023.

HAZONY, Yoram, *The Virtue of Nationalism*, New York, Basic Books, 2018.

HAZONY, Yoram, *Conservatism: A Rediscovery*, Washington, Regnery, 2022.

HEATH, Joseph, POTTER, Andrew, *The Rebel Sell: Why the Culture Can't be Jammed*, New York, Harper, [2004] 2010.

HENDERSON, Rob, *Troubled. A Memoir of Foster Care, Family, and Social Class*, New York, Gallery Books, 2024.

HIRSI ALI, Ayaan, *Prey. Immigration, Islam and the Erosion of Women's Rights*, New York, Harper, 2021.

HONEYWELL, Carissa, *Anarchism*, Cambridge, Polity, 2021.

INGLEHART, Ronald, *The Silent Revolution. Changing Values and Political Styles Among Western Publics*, Princeton, Princeton University Press, 1977.

JUDIS, John, TEXEIRA, Ruy, *The Emerging Democratic Majority*, New York, Scribner, 2002.

JULLIARD, Jacques, *Chronique du déclin français*, Paris, Albin Michel, 2023.

KANT, Immanuel, *Groundwork of the Metaphysics of Morals*, Cambridge, Cambridge University Press, [1785] 1997.

KAUFMANN, Eric, *Whiteshift. Populism, Immigration and the Future of White Majorities*, New York, Abrams Press, 2019.

KAUFMANN, Eric, *The Third Awokening. A 12-Point Plan for Rolling Back Progressive Extremism*, New York, Bombardier Press, 2024.

KELLY, Mark G. E., *Normal Now. Individualism as Conformity*, Cambridge, Polity, 2022.

KENDALL, Willmoore, *John Locke and the Doctrine of Majority-Rule*, Champaign, University of Illinois Press, 1959.

KLEIN, Naomi, *Doppelganger. A Trip Into the Mirror World*, Toronto, Knopf, 2023.

KOTKIN, Joel, *The Coming of Neo-Feudalism. A Warning to the Global Middle Class*, New York, Encounter, 2023.

KROPOTKIN, Petr, *Anarchist Morality*, Anarchist FAQ, 1891. https://anarchistfaq.org/translations/anarchist-morality.html.

KRUGER, Danny, *Covenant. The New Politics of Home, Neighbourhood and Nation*, Londres, Forum, 2023.

KYMLICKA, Will, *Multicultural Citizenship: A Liberal Theory of Minority Rights*, Oxford, Oxford University Press, 1995.

LANCTÔT, Aurélie, *Personne ne s'excusera. Affranchir la justice féministe de la violence de l'État*, Montréal, Atelier 10, 2024.

LASCH, Christopher, *The Revolt of the Elites and the Betrayal of Democracy*, New York, W. W. Norton & Company, 1995.

LASCH, Christopher, *The Culture of Narcissism: American Life in an Age of Diminishing Expectations*, New York, Norton, [1979] 1991.

LE CORRE, Aziliz, *L'Enfant est l'avenir de l'homme*, Paris, Albin Michel, 2024.

LÉVY, Bernard-Henri, *Solitude d'Israël*, Paris, Grasset, 2024.

LIND, Michael, *The New Class War. Saving Democracy from the Managerial Elite*, New York, Penguin, 2020.

LIND, Michael, *Hell to Pay. How the Suppression of Wages Is Destroying America*, New York, Penguin, 2023.

LINDENBERG, Daniel, *Le Rappel à l'ordre. Enquête sur les nouveaux réactionnaires*, Paris, Seuil, 2002.

LINDSAY, James, PLUCKROSE, Helen, *Cynical Theories. How Activist Scholarship Made Everything about Race, Gender, and Identity—and Why This Harms Everybody*, Durham, Pitchstone, 2020.

LIPOVETSKY, Gilles, *Le Crépuscule du devoir. L'éthique indolore des nouveaux temps démocratiques*, Paris, Gallimard, coll. Folio, 1992.

LOCKE, John, *Two Treatises of Government*, McMaster University Archive of the History of Economic Thought, 1689. https://www.yorku.ca/comninel/courses/3025pdf/Locke.pdf.

LOCKE, John, *A Letter Concerning Toleration*. 1689.

MACK, Eric, *Libertarianism*, Cambridge, Polity, 2018.

MACINTYRE, Alasdair, *After Virtue. A Story in Moral Theory*, Notre Dame, University of Notre Dame Press, 1981.

MANDEVILLE, Laure, *Les Révoltés d'Occident. De Trump à Zemmour, que se passe-t-il vraiment?*, Paris, Observatoire, 2022.

MARCUSE, Herbert, *One-Dimensional Man. Studies in the Ideology of Advanced Industrial Society*, Boston, Beacon Press, [1964] 1991.

MARX, Karl, ENGELS, Friedrich, *The Communist Manifesto*, London, Penguin Books, [1848] 2002.

MICHÉA, Jean-Claude, *La Double pensée. Retour sur la question libérale*, Paris, Flammarion, coll. Champs, 2008.

MIDAL, Fabrice, *Sauvez votre peau! Devenez narcissiques*, Paris, Flammarion, 2017.

MILL, John Stuart, *On Liberty*, Kitchener, Batoche Books, [1859] 2001.

MILL, John Stuart, *On Liberty, Utilitarianism and Other Essays*, Oxford, Oxford University Press, 2015.

MILLER, Paul D., *The Religion of American Greatness. What's Wrong With Christian Nationalism*, Downers Grove, InterVarsity Press, 2022.

MOUFFE, Chantal, LACLAU, Ernesto, *Hégémo Hegemony and Socialist Strategy: Towards a Radical Democratic Politics*, London, Verso, 1985.

MOUNK, Yascha, *La Grande expérience. Les démocraties face à la diversité*, Paris, Observatoire, 2022.

MOUNK, Yascha, *The Identity Trap. A Story of Ideas and Power in Our Time*, Penguin, New York, 2023.

MÜLLER, Jan-Werner, *Qu'est-ce que le populisme?*, Paris, Gallimard, coll. Folio, 2016.

MURRAY, Douglas, *The War on the West. How to Prevail in the Age of Unreason*, Londres, HarperCollins, 2022.

NAULLEAU, Éric, ONFRAY, Michel, *La Gauche réfractaire*, Paris, Bouquins, 2022.

NASH, George H., *The Conservative Intellectual Movement in America Since 1945*, Wilmington, ISI Books, [1976] 2006.

NOZICK, Robert, *Anarchy, State and Utopia*, Oxford, Blackwell, 1974.

NUSSBAUM, Martha, *The New Religious Intolerance. Overcoming the Politics of Fear in an Anxious Age*, Cambridge, Harvard University Press, 2012.

OGIEN, Ruwen, *L'Éthique aujourd'hui. Maximalistes et minimalistes*, Paris, Gallimard, coll. Folio, 2007.

OGIEN, Ruwen, *L'État nous rend-il meilleurs?*, Paris, Gallimard, coll. Folio, 2013.

ONFRAY, Michel, *Décadence*, Paris, Flammarion, 2017.

ORTEGA Y GASSET, José, *The Revolt of the Masses*, New York, Norton, [1929] 1964.

ORWELL, George, *The Road to Wigan Pier*, New York, Penguin Books, [1937] 2014.

PAXTON, Robert, *The Anatomy of Fascism*, New York, Vintage, [2004] 2005.

PETHOKOUKIS, James, *The Conservative Futurist. How to Create the Sci-Fi World We Were Promised*, New York, Center Street, 2023.

PERRY, Louise, *The Case Against the Sexual Revolution*, Cambridge, Polity, 2022.

PINKER, Steven, *The Blank Slate. The Modern Denial of Human Nature*, New York, Penguin, [2002] 2016.

POPPER, Karl, *The Open Society and Its Enemies, volume 1: The Spell of Plato*, London, Routledge, 1945.

POTTER, Andrew, *On Decline: Stagnation, Nostalgia, and Why Every Year is the Worst One Ever*, Windsor, Biblioasis, 2021.

PUTNAM, Robert D., *Bowling Alone. The Collapse and Revival of American Community*, New York, Simon & Schuster, 2000.

PUTNAM, Robert D. avec ROMNEY GARRETT, Shaylyn, *The Upswing. How America Came Together a Century Ago and How We Can Do It Again*, New York, Simon & Schuster, 2020.

RAWLS, John, *Political Liberalism. Expanded Edition*, New York, Columbia University Press, [1993] 2005.

REDEKER, Robert, *Les Sentinelles d'humanité. Philosophie de l'héroïsme et de la sainteté*, Paris, Desclée de Brouwer, 2019.

REICH, Robert, *The Common Good*, New York, Vintage, 2018.

REICH, Wilhelm, *The Mass Psychology of Fascism*, New York, Orgone Institute Press, [1933] 1946.

REICHBERG, Emmanuel, DE GUERPEL, Wandrille, *Le Vrai coût du progressisme. Associations, médias, ONG, institutions, enquête sur un gouffre financier*, Paris, L'Artilleur, 2024.

REVEL, Jean-François, *La Connaissance inutile*, Paris, Grasset, 1988.

RICARD, François, *La Génération lyrique. Essai sur la vie et l'œuvre des premiers nés du baby-boom*, Montréal, Boréal, 1992.

RIEFF, Philip, *The Triumph of the Therapeutic. Uses of Faith After Freud*, Wilmington, ISI Books, [1966] 2006.

ROBERTS, Kevin, *Dawn's Early Light. Burning Down Washington to Save America*, New York, Broadside, 2004.

ROSA, Hartmut, *Aliénation et accélération. Vers une théorie critique de la modernité tardive*, Paris, La Découverte, coll. Poche, [2012] 2014.

ROTHMAN, Noah, *The Rise of the New Puritans. Fighting Back Against Progressives' War on Fun*, New York, Broadside, 2022.

ROUSSEAU, Jean-Jacques, *The Social Contract and The First and Second Discourses*, New Haven, Yale University Press, 2002.

RUBIN, Jeff, *The Expendables. How the Middle Class Got Screwed by Globalization*, Toronto, Vintage Canada, [2020] 2022.

RUFFINI, Patrick, *Party of the People. Inside the Multiracial Populist Coalition Remaking the GOP*, New York, Simon & Schuster, 2023.

RYAN, Christopher, *Civilized to Death. The Price of Progress*, New York, Avid Reader, [2019] 2020.

RYUN, Ned, *American Leviathan. The Birth of the Administrative State and Progressive Authoritarianism*, New York, Encounter, 2024.

SAINTE-MARIE, Jérôme, *Bloc populaire. Une subversion électorale inachevée*, Paris, Cerf, 2021.

SANDEL, Michael J., *La Tyrannie du mérite. Qu'avons-nous fait du bien commun?*, Paris, Albin Michel, [2020] 2021.

SARTRE, Jean-Paul, *Existentialism Is a Humanism*, Marxists Internet Archive, 1946, https://www.marxists.org/reference/archive/sartre/works/exist/sartre.htm.

SENNETT, Richard, *The Fall of Public Man. 40th Anniversary Edition*, New York, W. W. Norton & Company, [1974] 2017.

SCHNAPPER, Dominique (éd.), *Qu'est-ce que la citoyenneté?*, Paris, Gallimard, coll. Folio, 2000.

SCHUMPETER, Joseph, *Capitalism, Socialism, and Democracy*, New York, Harper, 1942.

SCHWARTZ, Howard, *The Revolt of the Primitive. An Inquiry Into the Roots of Political Correctness*, Westport, Praeger, 2001.

SCRUTON, Roger, *The Meaning of Conservatism*, South Bend, St. Augustine's Press, [1983] 2002.

SCRUTON, Roger, *How to Think Seriously About the Planet. The Case for an Environmental Conservatism*, Oxford, Oxford University Press, 2012.

SCRUTON, Roger, *Conservatism: An Invitation to the Great Tradition*, New York, All Points Books, [2017] 2018. Ebook edition.

SCRUTON, Roger, *A Political Philosophy. Arguments for Conservatism*, Londres, Bloomsbury, [2006] 2019.

SCRUTON, Roger, *Confessions of a Heretic*, Kendal, Notting Hill, [2016] 2021.

SCRUTON, Roger, *Against the Tide*, Londres, Bloomsbury, 2022.

SHELLENBERGER, Michael, *San Fransicko. Why Progressives Ruin Cities*, New York, Harper, 2021.

SIEYÈS, Emmanuel-Joseph, *Political Writings*, Indianapolis, Hackett, 2003.

SIMON-NAHUM, Perrine, *La Nouvelle causalité diabolique*, Paris, Observatoire, 2024.

SINGER, Peter, *Animal Liberation. The Definitive Classic of the Animal Movement*, New York, Ecco, [1975] 2009.

SINGER, Peter, *The Expanding Circle. Ethics, Evolution and Moral Progress*, Princeton, Princeton University Press, [1981] 2011.

SPOONER, Lysander, *No Treason. The Constitution of No Authority*, Amazon, [1870] 2010, édition Kindle.

STANLEY, Jason, *How Fascism Works. The Politics of Us and Them*, New York, Random House, [2018] 2020.

STEBENNE, David, *Promised Land. How the Rise of the Middle Class Transformed America, 1929-1968*, New York, Scribner, [2020] 2021.

SUGY, Paul, *L'Extinction de l'homme. Le projet fou des antispécistes*, Paris, Tallandier, 2021.

TAGUIEFF, Pierre-André, *Le Sens du progrès.Une approche historique et philosophique*, Paris, Flammarion, coll. Champs, 2004.

TAGUIEFF, Pierre-André, *Les Nietzschéens et leurs ennemis.Pour, avec et contre Nietzsche*, Paris, Cerf, 2021.

TAGUIEFF, Pierre-André, *Le Retour de la décadence. Penser l'époque postprogressiste*, Paris, PUF, 2022.

TAMIR, Yael, *Why Nationalism*, Princeton, Princeton University Press, [2019] 2020.

TAUSSIG, Sylvie, *Le Système du complotisme*, Paris, Bouquins, 2021.

TAYLOR, Charles, *Multiculturalism: Examining the Politics of Recognition*, Princeton, Princeton University Press, 1994.

TODD, Emmanuel, *Où en sommes-nous? Une esquisse de l'histoire humaine*, Paris, Seuil, 2017.

TRUEMAN, Carl, *Strange New World. How Thinkers and Activists Redefined Identity and Sparked the Sexual Revolution*, Wheaton, Crossway, 2022.

TWENGE, Jean M., *Generations. The Real Differences Between Gen Z, Millennials, Gen X, Boomers, and Silents—and What They Mean for America's Future*, New York, Atria, 2023.

VALENTIN, Pierre, *Comprendre la révolution woke*, Paris, Gallimard, coll. Le Débat, 2023.

VANCE, J. D., *Hillbilly Elegy. A Memoir of a Family and Culture in Crisis*, New York, Harper [2016] 2018.

VERMEULE, Adrian, *Common Good Constitutionalism*, Cambridge, Polity, 2022.

WALLIS SIMONS, Jake, *Israelophobia. The Newest Version of the Oldest Hatred*, Londres, Constable, 2023.

WEIL, Simone, *The Need for Roots: Prelude to a Declaration of Duties towards Mankind*, New York, Routledge, [1949] 2002.

WILCOX, Brad, *Get Married. Why Americans Must Defy the Elites, Forge Strong Families, and Save Civilization*, New York, Broadside, 2024.

WOLFF, Robert Paul, MOORE, Barrington Jr MARCUSE, Herbert, *A Critique of Pure Tolerance*, Boston, Beacon Press, 1969.

WOODCOCK, George, *Anarchism: A History Of Libertarian Ideas And Movements*, Cleveland, Meridian, 1962.

Articles

AHMARI, Sohrab, "America's dime-store nietzscheans," *The New Statesman*, 16 May 2024.

APPLEBAUM, Yoni, "Why Donald Trump supporters are voting alone," *The Atlantic*, 7 April 2016.

BARBARIT, Simon, DAVID, Romain, "Loi immigration: le Conseil constitutionnel censure très largement le texte," *Public Sénat*, 25 January 2024

BASHIR, Martin, "General election 2019: Chief rabbi attacks Labour anti-Semitism record," *BBC*, 26 November 2019.

BASTIÉ, Eugénie, "Nouvelle-Calédonie: la gauche contre "le grand remplacement" . . . des Kanaks," *Le Figaro*, 17 May 2024.

BOLLAG, Sophia, "Gavin Newsom is tacking rightward on crime—and he's not the only one," *San Francisco Chronicle*, 19 March 2024.

BROWNSTONE, Sydney, CLARRIDGE, Christine, GUTMAN, David, BEEKMAN, Daniel, "Shooting at Seattle's CHOP protest site kills 16-year-old boy, leaves 14-year-old seriously injured," *Seattle Times*, 29 June 2020.

CAIN, Patrick, "Young voters favour Conservatives over other parties: poll," *Ipolitics*, 14 December 2022.

CHMIELEWSKI, Dawn, "The 68 companies (including Apple) that are taking North Carolina's anti-LGBT law to court," *Vox*, 8 July 2016.

CONRUYT, Claire, "UE: un nouvel amendement de Bellamy contre la promotion du voile par les institutions européennes, finalement adopté," *Le Figaro*, 19 October 2022.

COX, Daniel A., "The State of American Friendship: Change, Challenges, and Loss," *Survey Center on American Life*, 8 June 2021.

DATAN, "L'origine sociale des députés," 2024, https://datan.fr/statistiques/deputes-origine-sociale.

DENEEN, Patrick J., "A Good That Is Common," *Postliberal Order*, 8 November 2021.

DEVECCHIO, Alexandre, "Mathieu Bock-Côté: 'La droitisation antiwoke des jeunes hommes est visible partout en Occident'," *Le Figaro*, 15 November 2024.

FERRAND, Olivier, PRUDENT, Romain, JEANBART, Bruno, "Gauche: quelle majorité électorale pour 2012 ?," *Fondation Terra Nova*, 10 May 2011

FORREST, Adam, "Civil servants hold 'Remain bias' and resist Brexit reforms, claims UK attorney general," *The Independent*, 4 July 2022.

FOURQUET, Jérôme, "La fin de la grande classe moyenne," *Fondation Jean-Jaurès*, 16 May 2019.

GENTILHOMME, Célestine, "Israël-Hamas: Mélenchon accuse Braun-Pivet de "'camper à Tel Aviv pour encourager le massacre,'" *Le Figaro*, 22 October 2023.

GOWDY, J. David, "Without Virtue There Can Be No Liberty," *The Washington, Jefferson & Madison Institute*, 3 April 2011.

IQBAL, Nosheen, "Woke washing? How brands like Gillette turn profits by creating a conscience," *The Guardian*, 19 January 2019.

JOHANNÈS, Frank, "Comment le Rassemblement national est devenu le premier parti de la génération des 25-34 ans," *Le Monde*, 5 April 2021.

KAUFMANN, Eric, "Academic Freedom in Crisis: Punishment, Political Discrimination, and Self-Censorship," *Center for the Study of Partisanship and Ideology*, 1 March 2021.

KHEIRIDDIN, Tasha, "Canada's multicultural utopia now a balkanized grievance factory," *National Post*, 7 November 2023.

KYEYUNE, Malcom, "France's Bread Riots," *Compact*, 6 July 2023.

LUKIANOFF, Greg, SCHLOTT, Rikki, "Universities Use DEI Statements to Enforce Groupthink," *Reason*, February 2024.

MARQUIS, Mélanie, CHOUINARD, Tommy, "Baisse des seuils d'immigration permanente. 'Une pause responsable et pragmatique,' plaide Justin Trudeau," *La Presse*, 24 October 2024.

MAZUY, Magali, BARBIERI, Magali, BRETON, Didier, D'ALBIS, Hippolyte, "Les hommes ont des enfants plus tard que les femmes," *Institut national d'études démographiques*, March 2016.

PUTNAM, Robert D., "E Pluribus Unum: Diversity and Community in the Twenty-first Century," *Scandinavian Political Studies*, vol. 30(2), 2007, pp. 137–174.

RADIO-CANADA, "Des agents antirumeurs pour briser les préjugés envers les immigrants," 26 April 2018.

ROMANO, Aja, "#BlackoutTuesday derailed #BlackLivesMatter. A community organizer explains how to do better," *Vox*, 3 June 2020.

ROSENCHER, Anne, "Après Cologne, des féministes 'dans le déni' pour Elisabeth Badinter," *Marianne*, 21 January 2016.

ROSENTIEL, Tom, "Young Voters in the 2008 Election," *Pew Research Center*, 13 November 2008.

ROZADO, David, AL-GHARBI, Musa, HALBERSTADT, Jamin, "Prevalence of Prejudice-Denoting Words in News Media Discourse: A Chronological Analysis," *Social Science Comptuer Review*, 41(1), July 2021, pp. 99–122.

SANDERS, Linley, "How 5 key demographic groups voted in 2024: AP VoteCast," *Associated Press*, 7 November 2024.

SHASHKEVICH, Alex, "Meeting online has become the most popular way US couples connect, Stanford sociologist finds," *Stanford Review*, 21 August 2019.

SCHMITZ, Matthew, "Nietzscheans and Normies," *The American Conservative*, 14 August 2023.

SEAL, Thomas, "BC rolls back drug decriminalization after public backlash," *National Post*, 28 April 2024.

SEARLES, Michael, "Labour moves to ban puberty blockers permanently," *The Telegraph*, 12 July 2024.

SHERMAN, Carter, "'A big cratering:' an expert on Gen Z's surprise vote—and young women's growing support for Trump," *The Guardian*, 8 November 2024.

SICARD, Natalie, "L'application Partage Club: emprunter des objets à ses voisins au lieu de les acheter," *Journal de Montréal*, 28 April 2024.

SOLZHENITSYN, Aleksandr, "A World Split Apart," *The Alexander Solzhenitsyn Center*, https://www.solzhenitsyncenter.org/a-world-split-apart.

SOJIT PECHJA, Camille, "Better living through anarchy: Tracking the rise of the temporary autonomous zone," *Document Journal*, 19 August 2020.

SYAL, Rajeev, "Civil servants obliged to carry out Tory Rwanda deportations, court rules," *The Guardian*, 5 July 2024.

THE CIVIL SERVANT, "After years of being gaslit by government, we civil servants can breathe again under Labour," *The Guardian*, 12 July 2024.

THE NEW YORK TIMES, "Kindly Greeting Held Way To Convert Nazi Invaders," April 2, 1937.

THÉVENIAUD, Pauline, "Convention citoyenne sur la fin de vie: Macron et le gouvernement veulent dépolitiser le débat," *Le Parisien*, 4 December 2022.

TRUONG, Nicolas, "Giorgio Agamben: 'L'épidémie montre clairement que l'état d'exception est devenu la condition normale,'" *Le Monde*, 24 March 2020.

UK EQUALITY AND HUMAN RIGHTS COMMISSION, "Investigation into antisemitism in the Labour Party," October 2020.

VALENTIN, Pierre, "Une crèche Anne Frank veut changer de nom, ou le point d'orgue de l'idéologie de la déconstruction," *Le Figaro*, 8 November 2023.

VALENTIN, Pierre, "L'individualisme thérapeutique," *Fondation Jean-Jaurès*, à paraître.

VANEK SMITH, Stacey, "Riots that followed anti-racism protests come at great cost to black-owned businesses," *National Public Radio*, 12 August 2020.

WILLIAMS, Zoe, "The men-are-trash narrative is back. But what if women are also trash?," *The Guardian*, 27 March 2023.

ZIVO, Adam, "'Almost as good as giving (drug users) cash'—Report slams 'safer supply'; of free opioids," *National Post*, 8 August 2024.

XERRI, Ambre, "CRIF et extrême droite: la classe politique s'insurge contre un énième 'dérapage' de Jean-Luc Mélenchon," *Le Figaro*, 17 July 2023.

Notes

Introduction

1 Pierre-André Taguieff, *Le Retour de la décadence*, pp. 9–10.
2 Raymond Aron, *50 ans de réflexion politique. Mémoires*, p. 680.
3 Jacques Julliard, *Chronique du déclin français*, p. 17.
4 Michael Lind, *The New Class War*, pp. 40–42.
5 Robert D. Putnam with Shaylyn Romney Garrett, *The Upswing*, p. 38–39.
6 Jérôme Fourquet, "La fin de la grande classe moyenne."
7 Jean M. Twenge, *Generations*, pp. 33–73.
8 Robert D. Putnam with Shaylyn Romney Garrett, *The Upswing*, pp. 175–176.
9 Hartmut Rosa, *Aliénation et accélération*, pp. 22–23, 99
10 Alexandre Devecchio, *Les Nouveaux enfants du siècle*, pp. 10, 227.
11 Simone Weil, *The Need for Roots*, p. 40.
12 Norbert Elias, *The Civilizing Process*.
13 Robert D. Putnam, "E *Pluribus Unum*: Diversity and Community in the Twenty-First Century," p. 137.
14 Ross Douthat, *The Decadent Society*.
15 Ronald Inglehart, *The Silent Revolution*.
16 Christopher Lasch, *The Revolt of the Elites and the Betrayal of Democracy*.

Chapter 1

1 Jean-Jacques Rousseau, *The Social Contract and the First and Second Discourses*, pp. 170, 172.
2 Emmanuel-Joseph Sieyès, *Political Writings*, pp. 94–96.
3 *Ibid.*, p. 99.
4 John Locke, *Two Treatises of Government*, p. 146.
5 On this subject, see Willmoore Kendall, *John Locke and the Doctrine of Majority Rule.*
6 John Locke, *A Letter Concerning Toleration.*
7 J. David Gowdy, "Without Virtue There Can Be No Liberty."
8 Emmanuel Kant, *Groundwork of the Metaphysics of Morals*, p. 31.
9 Sigmund Freud, *The Standard Edition of the Complete Psychological Works of Sigmund Freud, Volume XXI*, pp. 95, 112.
10 *Ibid.*, p. 142.
11 Norbert Elias, *La Civilisation des moeurs.*
12 Gilles Lipovetsky, *Le Crépuscule du devoir*, p. 14. Our translation.
13 *Ibid.*, p. 31.
14 Robert D. Putnam with Shaylyn Romney Garrett, *The Upswing*, pp. 176, 184.
15 Christophe Guilluy, *No Society*, p. 77. Our translation.
16 Eric Kaufmann, *Whiteshift*, pp. 502–503.
17 Joseph Heath and Andrew Potter, *The Rebel Sell*, p. 117.
18 Mark G. E. Kelly, *Normal Now*, pp. 2–4.
19 Laurent Bouvet, *Le Sens du peuple*, p. 110. Our translation.
20 Hannah Arendt, *Eichmann in Jerusalem*, chapter VIII: Duties of a Law-Abiding Citizen.
21 *Ibid.*, chapter II: The Accused.
22 *Ibid.*, chapter III: An Expert on the Jewish Question.
23 Adolf Eichmann, quoted in Johann Chapoutot, *La Révolution culturelle nazie*, p. 241. Our translation.
24 *Ibid.*, p. 240.
25 *Ibid.*, p. 233.
26 Hannah Arendt, *Eichmann in Jerusalem*, chapter VI: The Final Solution: Killing.
27 *Ibid.*, Postscript.
28 *Ibid.*, chapter XV: Judgment, Appeal and Execution.
29 *Ibid.*, chapter VIII: Duties of a Law-Abiding Citizen.
30 Theodor W. Adorno, *The Authoritarian Personality.*
31 Wilhelm Reich, *The Mass Psychology of Fascism*, p. 24.

32 *Ibid.*, p. 44.
33 *Ibid.*, p. 71.
34 *Ibid.*, p. 46.
35 *Ibid.*, p. 88.
36 Geoffroy de Lagasnerie, *3. Une aspiration au dehors*, p. 21. Our translation.
37 Mona Chollet, *Résister à la culpabilité*, p. 109. Our translation.
38 *Ibid.*, p. 120.
39 Roger Scruton, *Conservatism*, chapter 2: The Birth of Philosophical Conservatism.
40 Howard Schwartz, *The Revolt of the Primitive*, chapter 2: "The Sexual Holy War and the Meaning of Work."
41 Jean-Jacques Rousseau, *The Social Contract and the First and Second Discourses*, p. 204.
42 John Locke, *Two Treatises of Government*, pp. 193, 202.
43 Camille Dejardin, *John Stuart Mill, libéral utopiste*, p. 189.
44 John Stuart Mill, *On Liberty*, p. 62.
45 *Ibid.*, pp. 8–9.
46 *Ibid.*, p. 31.
47 *Ibid.*, pp. 54–56.
48 *Ibid.*, p. 65.
49 *Ibid.*, p. 13.
50 Roger Scruton, *The Meaning of Conservatism*, pp. 31–32.
51 Karl Popper, *The Open Society and Its Enemies, volume 1: The Spell of Plato*, p. 145.
52 *Ibid.*, p. 151.
53 *Ibid.*, p. 153.
54 Mona Chollet, *Résister à la culpabilisation*, p. 137.
55 Karl Popper, *The Open Society and Its Enemies, volume 1: The Spell of Plato*, pp. 108–109.
56 Maroun Eddé, *La Mémoire coupable*, pp. 80–81.
57 Mathieu Bock-Côté, *Le Totalitarisme sans le goulag*, chapitre 1: "L'extrême-droite introuvable." Our translation.
58 Judith Butler, *Who's Afraid of Gender?*, p. 245.
59 Jason Stanley, *How Fascism Works*, p. 106.
60 *Ibid.*, pp. XI, 49–50.
61 *Ibid.*, pp. 110, 146, 178.
62 Philippe Marlière, "Un nouvel autoritarisme," in Bertrand Badie and Dominique Vidal (eds.), *Le Retour des populismes: l'état du monde 2019*, p. 103. Our translation.

63 *Ibid.*, p. 105.
64 *Ibid.*, p. 108.
65 Paul Gottfried, *Antifascism: The Course of a Crusade*, pp. 63–64.
66 Johann Chapoutot, *La Révolution culturelle nazie*, p. 14. Our translation.
67 *Ibid.*, pp. 77, 103, 295.
68 Robert Paxton, *The Anatomy of Fascism*, p. 130.
69 Johann Chapoutot, *La Révolution culturelle nazie*, p. 227.
70 Robert Paxton, *The Anatomy of Fascism*, p. 11.
71 Roger Griffin, *Fascism*, p. 10.
72 Joseph Goebbels, quoted in *ibid.*, p. 84.
73 Christophe Guilluy, *Le Crépuscule de la France d'en-haut*, pp. 176–177. Our translation.
74 Jérôme Fourquet, *Le Nouveau clivage*, pp. 50–54.
75 David Goodhart, *The Road to Somewhere.*
76 Christophe Guilluy, *Le Crépuscule de la France d'en-haut*, p. 203.
77 Jérôme Sainte-Marie, *Bloc populaire*, p. 63. Our translation.
78 Christophe Guilluy, *Les Dépossédés*, p. 124. Our translation.

Chapter 2

1 Isaiah Berlin, *Liberty*, p. 48.
2 John Stuart Mill, *On Liberty*, p. 87.
3 Camille Dejardin, *John Stuart Mill: Libéral utopiste*, p. 188.
4 Philip Rieff, *The Triumph of the Therapeutic*, p. 17.
5 *Ibid.*, p. 26.
6 Timothy P. Carney, *Family Unfriendly*, p. 258.
7 Geoffroy de Lagasnerie, *3. Une aspiration au dehors*, p. 203. Our translation.
8 *Ibid.*, pp. 47, 110–111.
9 *Ibid.*, p. 106.
10 Claude Habib, *Le Privé n'est pas politique*, p. 265. Our translation.
11 Geoffroy de Lagasnerie, *3. Une aspiration au dehors*, pp. 10–11. Our translation.
12 *Ibid.*, p. 75.
13 Mona Chollet, *Résister à la culpabilisation*, pp. 151, 154, 189. Our translation.
14 Geoffroy de Lagasnerie, *3. Une aspiration au dehors*, p. 58. Our translation.
15 *Ibid.*, pp. 78, 95.

16 Pierre Valentin, "L'individualisme thérapeutique."
17 Geoffroy de Lagasnerie, *3. Une aspiration au dehors*, pp. 48, 69. Our translation.
18 Eric Mack, *Libertarianism*, p. 1.
19 David Boaz, *The Libertarian Mind*, p. 39.
20 Joseph Heath and Andrew Potter, *The Rebel Sell*, p. 70.
21 David Boaz, *The Libertarian Mind*, p. 134.
22 Eric Mack, *Libertarianism*, p. 2.
23 Lysander Spooner, *No Treason*, Kindle edition, loc. 117.
24 George Woodcock, *Anarchism*, p. 234.
25 *Ibid.*, p. 32.
26 Carissa Honeywell, *Anarchism*, p. 21.
27 Petr Kropotkin, *Anarchist Morality*, VIII.
28 *Ibid.*, X.
29 *Ibid.*, I.
30 Vladimir Biaggi (ed.), *Le Nihilisme*, pp. 11, 14. Our translation.
31 Isaiah Berlin, *Liberty*, p. 195.
32 Eric Mack, *Libertarianism*, p. 90.
33 Camille Sojit Pejcha, "Better living through anarchy: Tracking the rise of the temporary autonomous zone."
34 Lysander Spooner, *No Treason*, loc. cit. 38.
35 *Ibid.*, loc. 142.
36 *Ibid.*, loc. 550.
37 Gracie May Bradley and Luke De Noronha, *Against Borders*, p. 3.
38 *Ibid.*, pp. 154–155.
39 Fabrice Midal, *Sauvez votre peau! Devenez narcissique*, p. 12.
40 *Ibid.*, p. 29. Our translation.
41 *Ibid.*, p. 101.
42 *Ibid.*, p. 63.
43 Mona Chollet, *Résister à la culpabilisation*, pp. 16, 18. Our translation.
44 *Ibid.*, p. 212.
45 Luc Ferry, *La Frénésie du bonheur*, p. 296.
46 Fabrice Midal, *Sauvez votre peau! Devenez narcissique*, p. 145. Our translation.
47 Jean M. Twenge, *Generations*, p. 173.
48 *Ibid.*, p. 243.
49 Anne Case and Angus Deaton, *Deaths of Despair and the Future of Capitalism*.
50 Jean M. Twenge, *Generations*, p. 136.

51 Theodore Dalrymple, *Admirable Evasions*, p. 81.
52 Peter Singer, *The Expanding Circle*, pp. 145–146.
53 John Stuart Mill, *On Liberty, Utilitarianism and Other Essays*, p. 121.
54 Christopher Lasch, *The Culture of Narcissism*, pp. 73–74.
55 Karl Marx, quoted in Luc Ferry, *La Frénésie du bonheur*, p. 220. Our translation.
56 *Ibid.*, pp. 9–10.
57 Mona Chollet, *Résister à la culpabilité*, p. 181.
58 Raymond Aron, *Plaidoyer pour l'Europe décadente*, p. 523.
59 Luc Ferry, *The Frenzy of Happiness*, pp. 243, 259.
60 Robert Nozick, *Anarchy, State, and Utopia*, p. 43.
61 Christopher Ryan, *Civilized to Death*, pp. 164–165.
62 *Ibid.*, p. 51.
63 Carissa Honeywell, *Anarchism*, pp. 74–75.
64 Thomas Seal, "B.C. rolls back drug decriminalization after public backlash."
65 Michael Shellenberger, *San Fransicko*, p. 49.
66 Adam Zivo, "Almost as good as giving (drug users) 'cash'–Report slams 'safer supply' of free opioids."
67 Michael Shellenberger, *San Fransicko*, p. 120.
68 Carissa Honeywell, *Anarchism*, p. 96.
69 Aurélie Lanctôt, *Personne ne s'excusera. Affranchir la justice féministe de la violence de l'État.*
70 Stacey Vanek Smith, "Riots that followed anti-racism protests come at great cost to black-owned businesses."
71 Sydney Brownstone, Christine Clarridge, David Gutman, and Daniel Beekman, "Shooting at Seattle's CHOP protest site kills 16-year-old boy, leaves 14-year-old seriously injured."
72 François-Xavier Bellamy, *Espérer*, p. 63. Our translation.
73 *The New York Times*, "Kindly Greeting Held Way to Convert Nazi Invaders," April 2, 1937.
74 Louise Perry, *The Case Against the Sexual Revolution*, p. 179.
75 *Ibid.*, p. 48.
76 Eugénie Bastié, *Le Porc émissaire*, pp. 124–126. Our translation.
77 Louise Perry, *The Case Against the Sexual Revolution*, p. 52.
78 Ruwen Ogien, *L'État nous rend-t-il meilleurs?*, p. 207. Our translation.
79 *Ibid.*, pp. 231–232.
80 Camille Dejardin, *John Stuart Mill: Libéral utopiste*, p. 231. Our translation.

81 Manon Garcia, *La Conversation des sexes*, p. 138. Our translation.
82 Louise Perry, *The Case Against the Sexual Revolution*, p. 122.
83 Ruwen Ogien, *L'Éthique aujourd'hui*, p. 184.
84 Brad Wilcox, *Get Married*, pp. 64–69.
85 *Ibid.*, pp. 6–7.
86 Karl Popper, *The Open Society and Its Enemies, Volume 1: The Spell of Plato*, p. 107.
87 Sohrab Ahmari, *Tyranny Inc.*, p. XIX.
88 *Ibid.*, p. XXV.
89 Eugénie Bastié, *Le Porc émissaire*, p. 122. Our translation.
90 Patrick J. Deneen, *Regime Change*, pp. 6–7.
91 Gilbert Keith Chesterton, *Heretics*, p. 41.
92 Steven Pinker, *The Blank Slate*, p. 57.
93 *Ibid.*, p. 316.
94 *Ibid.*, p. 368.
95 Richard Dawkins, quoted in Christopher Ryan, *Civilized to Death*, p. 79.
96 Yael Tamir, *Why Nationalism*, pp. 44–45.
97 Zygmunt Bauman, *Liquid Life*, p. 27.
98 Rob Henderson, *Troubled*, chapter 11: "Luxury Beliefs."
99 Matthew B. Crawford, *The World Beyond Your Head*, p. 109.
100 *Ibid.*, p. 26.
101 Matthew B. Crawford, *Shop Class as Soulcraft*, p. 51.

Chapter 3

1 Joseph Heath and Andrew Potter, *The Rebel Sell*, pp. 31–32.
2 Mathieu Bock-Côté, *Le Multiculturalisme comme religion politique*, p. 100.
3 Michel Foucault, *Discipline and Punish*, p. 193.
4 *Ibid.*, pp. 207–208.
5 *Ibid.*, p. 222.
6 *Ibid.*, p. 228.
7 *Ibid.*, p. 276.
8 Zygmunt Bauman, *Strangers at Our Door*, p. 41.
9 Michel Foucault, *Discipline and Punish*, p. 289.
10 Joseph Heath and Andrew Potter, *The Rebel Sell*, p. 146.
11 Geoffroy de Lagasnerie, *3. Une aspiration au dehors*, p. 11.
12 Carl Trueman, *Strange New World*, p. 22.

13 Charles Taylor, *Multiculturalism*, p. 30.
14 *Ibid.*, p. 25.
15 Carl Trueman, *Strange New World*, p. 23.
16 Norbert Elias, *The Society of Individuals*; Jacques Beauchemin, *La Société des identités.*
17 Ronald Dworkin, *Taking Rights Seriously.*
18 Jeremy Carl, *The Unprotected Class.*
19 Judith Butler, *Who's Afraid of Gender*, chapter 6: What About Sex?
20 *Ibid.*, introduction: Gender Ideology and the Fear of Destruction.
21 *Ibid.*, chapter 5: TERFs and British Matters of Sex.
22 James Lindsay and Helen Pluckrose, *Cynical Theories*, p. 172.
23 Martha Nussbaum, *The New Religious Intolerance*, p. 105.
24 *Ibid.*, p. 125.
25 *Ibid.*, p. 79.
26 Ruwen Ogien, *L'Éthique aujourd'hui*, p. 128.
27 *Ibid.*, p. 73.
28 *Ibid.*, p. 198.
29 Patrick J. Deneen, *Regime Change*, p. 50.
30 Radio-Canada, "Des agents antirumeurs pour briser les préjugés envers les immigrants."
31 Charles Taylor, *Multiculturalism*, p. 25.
32 Patrick J. Deneen, *Conserving America?*, p. 8.
33 Paul D. Miller, *The Religion of American Greatness*, p. 36.
34 *Ibid.*, p. 75.
35 Ruwen Ogien, *L'État nous rend-t-il meilleurs?*, p. 137. Our translation.
36 Yascha Mounk, *The Great Experiment*, p. 142.
37 Will Kymlicka, *Multicultural Citizenship*, p. 97.
38 Adrian Favell, *The Integration Nation*, pp. 2–3.
39 *Ibid.*, p. 14.
40 Christiane Taubira, quoted in Eugénie Bastié, "Nouvelle-Calédonie: la gauche contre le 'Grand Remplacement' . . . des Kanaks," *Le Figaro*, May 17, 2024.
41 John Stuart Mill, *On Liberty*, p. 55.
42 Marcel Gauchet, *Le Désenchantement du monde*, p. 328. Our translation.
43 Noah Rothman, *The Rise of the New Puritans*, p. X.
44 Olivier Babeau, *Éloge de l'hypocrisie*, pp. 10, 24. Our translation.
45 Étienne Rey, quoted in *ibid.*, p. 96.
46 *Ibid.*, p. 239.

47 Richard Sennett, *The Fall of Public Man*, chapter 6: Man as Actor.
48 Dominique Schnapper, *Qu'est-ce que la citoyenneté?*, p. 44. Our translation.
49 John Rawls, *Political Liberalism*, p. 137.
50 Adrian Favell, *The Integration Nation*, pp. 167–168.
51 Roger Scruton, *Confessions of a Heretic*, pp. 65–66.
52 Benedict Anderson, *Imagined Communities.*
53 Claude Habib, *Le Privé n'est pas politique*, p. 48.
54 David Rozado, Musa Al-Gharbi, and Jamin Halberstadt, "Prevalence of Prejudice-Denoting Words in News Media Discourse: A Chronological Analysis."
55 Aja Romano, "#BlackoutTuesday derailed #BlackLivesMatter. A community organizer explains how to do better."
56 Samuel Fitoussi, *Woke Fiction.*
57 Nosheen Iqbal, "Woke washing? How brands like Gillette turn profits by creating a conscience."
58 Olivier Babeau, *Éloge de l'hypocrisie*, p. 213. Our translation.
59 Éric Duhaime, *La Fin de l'homosexualité et le dernier gay*, Chapter 1: "Un gay bien ordinaire." Our translation.
60 Claude Habib, *Le Privé n'est pas politique*, p. 47. Our translation.
61 Robert D. Putnam with Shaylyn Romney Garrett, *The Upswing*, pp. 233–234.
62 *Ibid.*, p. 276.
63 *Ibid.*, p. 278.
64 Jean M. Twenge, *Generations*, p. 317.
65 Zoe Williams, "The men-are-trash narrative is back. But what if women are also trash?"
66 Mary Harrington, *Feminism Against Progress*, p. 87.

Chapter 4

1 Karl Marx and Friedrich Engels, *The Communist Manifesto*, p. 222.
2 *Ibid.*, p. 243.
3 Jurgen Habermas, quoted in Amaury Giraud, *Penser le conservatisme à gauche*, p. 54. Our translation.
4 Joseph Heath and Andrew Potter, *The Rebel Sell*, p. 58.
5 Herbert Marcuse, *One-Dimensional Man*, pp. 1, XLVI.
6 *Ibid.*, p. 31.
7 *Ibid.*, pp. 256–257.

8 Laurent Bouvet, *La Nouvelle question laïque*, pp. 35–36. Our translation.
9 Herbert Marcuse, "Repressive Tolerance," in Robert Paul Wolff, Barrington Moore Jr., and Herbert Marcuse, *A Critique of Pure Tolerance*, p. 107.
10 Mathieu Bock-Côté, *Le Multiculturalisme comme religion politique*, p. 93. Our translation.
11 Pierre Valentin, *Comprendre la révolution woke*, p. 25. Our translation.
12 Herbert Marcuse, *One-Dimensional Man*, p. 276.
13 Pierre Valentin, *Comprendre la révolution woke*, pp. 44, 132.
14 *Ibid.*, p. 204.
15 Chantal Mouffe and Ernesto Laclau, *Hegemony and Socialist Strategy*.
16 Yves Bonnardel, Thomas Lepeltier, and Pierre Sigler (eds.), *La Révolution antispéciste*, p. 316. Our translation.
17 Luc Ferry and Alain Renaut, *La Pensée 68*, p. 88. Our translation.
18 Paul Sugy, *L'Extinction de l'homme*, p. 108. Our translation.
19 Yascha Mounk, *The Identity Trap*, p. 211.
20 Roger Scruton, *Against the Tide*, p. 187.
21 Yascha Mounk, *The Identity Trap*, p. 138.
22 Michel Foucault, quoted in Luc Ferry and Alain Renaut, *La Pensée 68*, p. 56. Our translation.
23 *Ibid.*, p. 58.
24 *Ibid.*, p. 263.
25 Robin DiAngelo, *White Fragility*.
26 James Lindsay and Helen Pluckrose, *Cynical Theories*, p. 140.
27 *Ibid.*, pp. 35–36.
28 All these expressions can be found in the titles of recently published essays.
29 Nicolas Truong, "Giorgio Agamben: 'L'épidémie montre clairement que l'état d'exception est devenu la condition normale.'"
30 Naomi Klein, *Doppelganger*, pp. 228–229.
31 Raymond Aron, *Plaidoyer pour l'Europe décadente*, pp. 179–180.
32 François-Xavier Bellamy, *Espérer*, p. 47. Our translation.
33 René Girard, *I See Satan Fall Like Lightning*, p. 161.
34 Bradley Campbell and Jason Manning, *The Rise of Victimhood Culture*, pp. 22, 24.
35 Jonathan Haidt, *The Righteous Mind.*
36 Douglas Murray, *The War on the West*, p. 34.
37 Robert Redeker, *The Sentinels of Humanity*, p. 15.
38 René Girard, *I See Satan Fall Like Lightning*, p. 164.

39 Yascha Mounk, *The Identity Trap*, p. 25.
40 Mathieu Bock-Côté, *Le Multiculturalisme comme religion politique*, pp. 108, 116. Our translation.
41 Peter Singer, *The Expanding Circle*, p. 120.
42 Peter Singer, *Animal Liberation*, p. 3.
43 Yves Bonnardel, Thomas Lepeltier, and Pierre Sigler (eds.), *La Révolution antispéciste*, p. 154. Our translation.
44 Sue Donaldson and Will Kymlicka, *Zoopolis*, p. 33.
45 *Ibid.*, p. 2.
46 Peter Singer, *The Expanding Circle*, p. 121.
47 Yves Bonnardel, Thomas Lepeltier, and Pierre Sigler (eds.), *La Révolution antispéciste*, p. 132. Our translation.
48 Sophie Durocher, *Où sont les femmes ?*, p. 22. Our translation.
49 Ayaan Hirsi Ali, *Prey*, p. XII.
50 Anne Rosencher, "Après Cologne, des féministes 'dans le déni' pour Elisabeth Badinter."
51 Judith Butler, *Who's Afraid of Gender?*, introduction: Gender Ideology and the Fear of Destruction.
52 Judith Butler, quoted in Pierre Valentin, *Comprendre la révolution woke*, p. 150. Our translation.
53 Judith Butler, *Who's Afraid of Gender?*, chapter 5: TERFs and British Matters of Sex.
54 *Ibid.*, chapter 5: TERFs and British Matters of Sex.
55 Sophie Durocher, *Où sont les femmes?*, p. 24. Our translation.
56 Perrine Simon-Nahum, *La Nouvelle causalité diabolique*, pp. 38–49.
57 Jake Wallis Simons, *Israelophobia: The Newest Version of the Oldest Hatred*, p. 180.
58 Michel Foucault, quoted in Michel Onfray, *Decadence*, pp. 551, 553. Our translation.
59 Célestine Gentilhomme, "Israël-Hamas: Mélenchon accuse Braun-Pivet de 'camper à Tel Aviv pour encourager le massacre.'" Our translation.
60 Ambre Xerri, "CRIF et extrême droite: la classe politique s'insurge contre un énième 'dérapage' de Jean-Luc Mélenchon."
61 UK Equality and Human Rights Commission, "Investigation into antisemitism in the Labour Party."
62 Martin Bashir, "General election 2019: Chief rabbi attacks Labour anti-Semitism record."
63 Bernard-Henri Lévy, *Solitude d'Israël*, p. 101. Our translation.

64 Yoram Hazony, *The Virtue of Nationalism*, pp. 214, 215.
65 Linley Sanders, "How 5 key demographic groups voted in 2024: AP Vote Cast."
66 John Judis and Ruy Texeira, *The Emerging Democratic Majority*.
67 Ross Douthat and Reihan Salam, *Grand New Party*, chapter 8: "Up from Compassion."
68 Darrell Bricker and John Ibbitson, *The Big Shift*, p. 231.
69 Darrell Bricker and John Ibbitson, *The Big Shift*, p. 236.
70 Eric Kaufmann, *Whiteshift*, pp. 444–449.
71 Patrick Ruffini, *Party of the People*, pp. 205–206.
72 *Ibid.*, pp. 103–105.
73 Raymond Aron, *Plaidoyer pour l'Europe décadente*, p. 58. Our translation.
74 Musa Al-Gharbi, *We Have Never Been Woke*, pp. 270, 296.
75 *Ibid.*, pp. 283–284.
76 *Ibid.*, p. 120.
77 Laurent Bouvet, *Le Sens du peuple*, p. 278. Our translation.

Chapter 5

1 Christopher Lasch, *The Revolt of the Elites and the Betrayal of Democracy*, p. 20.
2 James Burnham, *The Managerial Revolution*, p. 66.
3 *Ibid.*, p. 86.
4 Emmanuel Todd, *Où en sommes-nous?*, chapter 12: La démocratie minée par l'éducation supérieure.
5 *Ibid.*
6 Michael Lind, *Hell to Pay*, pp. 92–93.
7 Christopher Lasch, *The Revolt of the Elites and the Betrayal of Democracy*, p. 5.
8 *Ibid.*
9 Eric Kaufmann, "Academic Freedom in Crisis: Punishment, Political Discrimination, and Self-Censorship."
10 Eric Kaufmann, *The Third Awakening*, p. 162.
11 Judith Butler, *Who's Afraid of Gender?*, introduction: Gender Ideology and the Fear of Destruction.
12 David Brooks, *Bobos in Paradise*, p. 33.
13 Christopher Lasch, *The Revolt of the Elites and the Betrayal of Democracy*, p. 20.

14 Richard Florida, *The Rise of the Creative Class*, p. 10.
15 *Ibid.*, p. 293.
16 Robert Putnam, "*E Pluribus Unum*: Diversity and Community in the Twenty-first Century."
17 Richard Florida, *The Rise of the Creative Class*, pp. 255–256.
18 David Brooks, *Bobos in Paradise*, p. 26.
19 David Goodhart, *Head, Hand, Heart*, p. 4.
20 Michael J. Sandel, *The Tyranny of Merit*.
21 Richard Florida, *The Rise of the Creative Class*, p. 294.
22 David Brooks, *Bobos in Paradise*, p. 47.
23 Greg Lukianoff and Rikki Schlott, "Universities Use DEI Statements to Enforce Groupthink."
24 Musa Al-Gharbi, *We Have Never Been Woke*, p. 196.
25 Richard Florida, *The Rise of the Creative Class*, p. 400.
26 *Ibid.*, pp. 66–67.
27 *Ibid.*, p. 385.
28 David Goodhart, *Head, Hand, Heart*, p. 103.
29 *Ibid.*, pp. 148–149.
30 Michael Lind, *Hell to Pay*, p. 102.
31 Jérôme Fourquet, "La fin de la grande classe moyenne."
32 David Stebenne, *Promised Land*, pp. 125, 253.
33 *Ibid.*, pp. XI, 219, 236.
34 *Ibid.*, p. 252.
35 Patrick Ruffini, *Party of the People*.
36 Joel Kotkin, *The Coming of Neo-Feudalism*, p. 80.
37 David Stebenne, *Promised Land*, pp. 26–32.
38 *Ibid.*, p. 43.
39 Emmanuel Todd, *Où en sommes-nous ?*, chapter 12: La démocratie minée par l'éducation supérieure.
40 Joel Kotkin, *The Coming of Neo-Feudalism*, p. 13.
41 Richard Florida, *The Rise of the Creative Class*, p. 47.
42 Joel Kotkin, *The Coming of Neo-Feudalism*, pp. 129–130.
43 James Pethokoukis, *The Conservative Futurist*, pp. 221–222.
44 Jeff Rubin, *The Expendables*, p. 82.
45 Michael Lind, *The New Class War*.
46 David Brooks, *Bobos in Paradise*, p. 53.
47 Christophe Guilluy, *No Society*, p. 19.
48 Alexis de Tocqueville, *Democracy in America, Volume 1*, chapter 12: Political Associations in the United States.

49 Robert D. Putnam, *Bowling Alone.*
50 Michael Lind, *Hell to Pay*, p. 102.
51 Emmanuel Reichberg and Wandrille de Guerpel, *Le Vrai coût du progressisme*, p. 291.
52 Ned Ryun, *American Leviathan*, pp. 14–15, 22–23.
53 Adam Forrest, "Civil servants hold 'Remain bias' and resist Brexit reforms, claims UK attorney general."
54 Rajeev Syal, "Civil servants obliged to carry out Tory Rwanda deportations, court rules."
55 The Civil Servant, "After years of being gaslit by government, we civil servants can breathe again under Labour."
56 Ned Ryun, *American Leviathan*, pp. 56, 74.
57 Musa Al-Gharbi, *We Have Never Been Woke*, pp. 63–64.
58 Pauline Théveniaud, "Convention citoyenne sur la fin de vie: Macron et le gouvernement veulent dépolitiser le débat."
59 Richard Hanania, *The Origins of Woke*, p. 30.
60 *Ibid.*, pp. 13–14.
61 Simon Barbarit and Romain David, "Loi immigration: le Conseil constitutionnel censure très largement le texte."
62 Anne De Guigné, *Le Capitalisme woke*, p. 123. Our translation.
63 Dawn Chmielewski, "The 68 companies (including Apple) that are taking North Carolina's anti-LGBT law to court."
64 Anne De Guigné, *Le Capitalisme woke*, p. 37. Our translation.
65 *Ibid.*, p. 77.
66 *Ibid.*, p. 74.
67 Laurent Bouvet, *Le Sens du peuple*, p. 178. Our translation.
68 Patrick Deneen, *Regime Change*, chapter 3: "A Good That Is Common."
69 Eric Kaufmann, *The Third Awakening*, pp. 336–339.
70 Alexandre Devecchio, "Mathieu Bock-Côté: 'La droitisation antiwoke des jeunes hommes est visible partout en Occident.'"

Chapter 6

1 Jan-Werner Müller, *What Is Populism?*, introduction: Is Everyone a Populist?
2 George H. Nash, *The Conservative Intellectual Movement in America Since 1945*, pp. 76–77.
3 Kevin Roberts, *Dawn's Early Light*, p. 74.

4 J. D. Vance, in Kevin Roberts, *Dawn's Early Light*, p. XI.
5 *Ibid.*, p. 2.
6 José Ortega y Gasset, *The Revolt of the Masses*, p. 115.
7 J. D. Vance, *Hillbilly Elegy*, pp. 188–189.
8 Bradley Manning and Jason Campbell, *The Rise of Victimhood Culture*, p. 165.
9 Jonathan Haidt, *The Righteous Mind*, pp. 153–158.
10 Christophe Guilluy, *No Society*, p. 94.
11 Eugénie Bastié, *La Guerre des idées*, p. 18. Our translation.
12 Éric Naulleau and Michel Onfray, *La Gauche réfractaire*, p. 27. Our translation.
13 Amaury Giraud, *Penser le conservatisme à gauche*, p. 17. Our translation.
14 See Jean-Claude Michéa, *La Double pensée*.
15 Amaury Giraud, *Penser le conservatisme à gauche*, p. 244. Our translation.
16 Daniel Lindenberg, *Le Rappel à l'ordre*.
17 Eugénie Bastié, *La Dictature des ressentis*, p. 108. Our translation.
18 Laurent Bouvet, *Le Sens du peuple*, pp. 65–71.
19 Christophe Guilluy, *Le Temps des gens ordinaires*, p. 149. Our translation.
20 Laurent Bouvet, *Le Sens du peuple*, p. 73. Our translation.
21 *Ibid.*, p. 278.
22 Amaury Giraud, *Penser le conservatisme à gauche*, pp. 352–353. Our translation.
23 Jacques Julliard, *Chronique du déclin français*, pp. 356–357. Our translation.
24 Alexandre Devecchio, *Les Nouveaux enfants du siècle*, p. 224. Our translation.
25 Jérôme Sainte-Marie, *Bloc populaire*, p. 202. Our translation.
26 Marc Crapez, *Je suis un contrariant*. Our translation.
27 Yascha Mounk, *The Identity Trap*, p. 281.
28 Sylvie Taussig, *Le Système du complotisme*, pp. 22–23. Our translation.
29 Carl Trueman, *Strange New World*, p. 47.
30 Alexandre Devecchio, *Recomposition*, pp. 148–149.
31 Christopher Caldwell, *The Age of Entitlement*, p. 93.
32 Andrew Potter, *On Decline*, chapter 3: On Politics.
33 Pierre Valentin, *Comprendre la révolution woke*, p. 215. Our translation.
34 Gilbert Keith Chesterton, *Orthodoxy*, chapter 7: The Eternal Revolution.
35 Sylvie Taussig, *Le système du complotisme*, pp. 140–141. Our translation.

36 Naomi Klein, *Doppelganger*, p. 122.
37 *Ibid.*, pp. 102, 123.
38 Jérôme Fourquet, *L'Archipel français*, pp. 116–120.
39 Michael Lind, *The New Class War*, p. 83.
40 Kevin Roberts, *Dawn's Early Light*, p. 183.
41 Jérôme Sainte-Marie, *Bloc populaire*, pp. 146, 202. Our translation.
42 Christophe Guilluy, *La France périphérique*, p. 80. Our translation.
43 Michael Lind, *The New Class War*, p. 164.
44 Malcom Kyeyune, "France's Bread Riots."
45 Antoine Cargoët, *Recréer le ciel*, pp. 180–181.
46 Jérôme Sainte-Marie, *Bloc populaire*, p. 147.
47 Jérôme Fourquet, *Le Nouveau clivage*, p. 138. Our translation.
48 Matthew Goodwin, *Voice, Values and Virtue*, p. 66.
49 *Ibid.*, p. 167.
50 Roger Eatwell and Matthew Goodwin, *National Populism*, pp. 275–276.
51 Patrick Buisson, *La Cause du peuple*.
52 Matthew Goodwin, *Voice, Values, Virtue*, p. 117.
53 Datan, "L'origine sociale des députés."
54 Pierre-André Taguieff, *Les Nietzschéens et leurs ennemis*, p. 308. Our translation.
55 *Ibid.*, p. 127.
56 Friedrich Nietzsche, in *ibid.*, p. 133.
57 *Ibid.*, p. 125.
58 Carl Trueman, *Strange New World*, p. 62.
59 Friedrich Nietzsche, in *Les Nietzschéens et leurs ennemis*, p. 133. Our translation.
60 Steven A. Ascheim, in *ibid.*, pp. 155–156.
61 Carl Trueman, *Strange New World*, p. 63.
62 Pierre-André Taguieff, *Les Nietzschéens et leurs ennemis*, p. 324. Our translation.
63 Sohrab Ahmari, "America's dime-store Nietzscheans."
64 Matthew Schmitz, "Nietzscheans and Normies."
65 Richard Spencer, quoted in *ibid.*
66 Pierre-André Taguieff, *Les Nietzschéens et leurs ennemis*, pp. 334, 336, 342–343, 350. Our translation.
67 Jean-François Lyotard, in *ibid.*, p. 133.
68 Stephen Harper, *Right Here, Right Now*, p. 79.
69 Chantal Delsol, *La Haine du monde*, pp. 9–10. Our translation.

Chapter 7

1 Anne Applebaum, *Twilight of Democracy*.
2 Patrick J. Deneen, *Regime Change*, p. 230.
3 Patrick J. Deneen, "A Good That Is Common."
4 Yael Tamir, *Why Nationalism*, p. 63.
5 Patrick J. Deneen, *Regime Change*, p. 93.
6 Pierre-André Taguieff, *Le Sens du progrès*, pp. 317–318. Our translation.
7 Danny Kruger, *Covenant*, pp. VII–VIII.
8 François-Xavier Bellamy, *Les Déshérités*, p. 205.
9 George Orwell, *The Road to Wigan Pier*.
10 Robert Reich, *The Common Good*, p. 10.
11 Jérôme Fourquet, *L'Archipel français*, pp. 444–445.
12 Jonathan Haidt, *The Righteous Mind*, pp. 165–169.
13 Anthony Annett, *Cathonomics*, p. 33.
14 David Goodhart, *The British Dream*, p. XXX–XXXI.
15 Jérôme Sainte-Marie, *Bloc populaire*, p. 152. Our translation.
16 Adrian Vermeule, *Common Good Constitutionalism*, pp. 24, 127.
17 Jean-Paul Sartre, *Existentialism Is a Humanism*.
18 Aristotle, *The Nicomachean Ethics*.
19 Alasdair MacIntyre, *After Virtue*, chapter 12: Aristotle's Account of the Virtues.
20 Adrian Vermeule, *Common Good Constitutionalism*, pp. 36–37.
21 Alexander Solzhenitsyn, "A World Split Apart."
22 Michael Shellenberger, *San Fransicko*, p. 2.
23 Claire Conruyt, "UE: un nouvel amendement de Bellamy contre la promotion du voile par les institutions européennes, finalement adopté."
24 Roger Scruton, *A Political Philosophy*, p. 1.
25 Amaury Giraud, *Penser le conservatisme à gauche*, p. 249. Our translation.
26 Patrick J. Deneen, *Regime Change*, pp. 220–221.
27 Alasdair MacIntyre, *After Virtue*.
28 Yoram Hazony, *Conservatism: A Rediscovery*, p. 1.
29 Laurent Bouvet, *La Nouvelle question laïque*, pp. 247–248. Our translation.
30 Aristotle, *The Nicomachean Ethics*.
31 Robert D. Putnam, "*E Pluribus Unum*: Diversity and Community in the Twenty-first Century."
32 Robert D. Putnam with Shaylyn Romney Garrett, *The Upswing*, pp. 296–297.

33 *Ibid.*, pp. 163, 181.
34 Tasha Kheiriddin, "Canada's Multicultural Utopia Now a Balkanized Grievance Factory."
35 Robert D. Putnam with Shaylyn Romney Garrett, *The Upswing*, pp. 15–203.
36 Dominique Schnapper (ed.), *Qu'est-ce que la citoyenneté ?*, pp. 148–149.
37 Vincent Coussedière, *Éloge de l'assimilation*, pp. 233–236.
38 Laure Mandeville, *Les Révoltés d'Occident*, p. 309. Our translation.
39 Patrick J. Deneen, *Regime Change*, p. 127.
40 Laurent Bouvet, *Le Sens du peuple*, pp. 40–41.
41 Patrick J. Deneen, *Regime Change*, p. 152.
42 Régis Debray, quoted in Amaury Giraud, *Penser le conservatisme à gauche*, p. 270. Our translation.
43 Joseph Schumpeter, *Capitalism, Socialism, and Democracy.*
44 Mark Halperin and John F. Harris, *The Way to Win: Taking the White House in 2008*, p. XIX.
45 Mélanie Marquis and Tommy Chouinard, "Baisse des seuils d'immigration permanente. 'Une pause responsable et pragmatique', plaide Justin Trudeau."
46 Michael Searles, "Labour moves to ban puberty blockers permanently."
47 Sophia Bollag, "Gavin Newsom is tacking rightward on crime—and he's not the only one."

Conclusion

1 François Ricard, *La Génération lyrique.*
2 Daniel A. Cox, "The State of American Friendship: Change, Challenges, and Loss."
3 Jean M. Twenge, *Generations*, p. 409.
4 *Ibid.*, pp. 370, 508.
5 François Cardinal and Éric Montigny (eds.), *La Révolution Z*, pp. 46–48.
6 Julien Gobin, *L'individu, fin de parcours ?*, p. 128. Our translation.
7 Alex Shashkevich, "Meeting online has become the most popular way U.S. couples connect, Stanford sociologist finds."
8 Natalie Sicard, "L'application Partage Club: emprunter des objets à ses voisins au lieu de les acheter."
9 Julien Gobin, *L'individu, fin de parcours?*, p. 130. Our translation.
10 Magali Mazuy, Magali Barbieri, Didier Breton, and Hippolyte d'Albis, "Les hommes ont des enfants plus tard que les femmes."

11 Jean M. Twenge, *Generations*, p. 421.
12 Allan Bloom, *The Closing of the American Mind.*
13 François-Xavier Bellamy, *Les Déshérités*, p. 201. Our translation.
14 Aziliz Le Corre, *L'Enfant est l'avenir de l'homme*, p. 127.
15 Alexandre Devecchio, *Les Nouveaux enfants du siècle*, p. 281.
16 Carter Sherman, "A big cratering: an expert on Gen Z's surprise votes—and young women's growing support for Trump."
17 Tom Rosentiel, "Young Voters in the 2008 Election."
18 Yoni Applebaum, "Why Donald Trump Supporters Are Voting Alone."
19 Frank Johannès, "Comment le Rassemblement national est devenu le premier parti de la génération des 25–34 ans."
20 Patrick Cain, "Young voters favor Conservatives over other parties: poll."
21 Patrick Deneen, *Why Liberalism Failed.*
22 Robert D. Putnam with Shaylyn Romney Garrett, *The Upswing.*
23 Michael J. Sandel, *The Tyranny of Merit*, p. 212.
24 Rod Dreher, *The Benedictict Option*, chapter 4: "A New Kind of Christian Politics."
25 Claude Habib, *Le Privé n'est pas politique*, p. 165.
26 Aziliz Le Corre, *L'Enfant est l'avenir de l'homme*, p. 236. Our translation.
27 Roger Scruton, *How to Think Seriously About the Planet*, p. 25.